The relationship between intellectual life and institutionalism is the grand theme of Jack Goody's new book. His focus is on the development of the discipline of social anthropology in Britain through its key practitioners and how far its concerns interact with the political and ideological debate of the interwar years. As such this is a study of the different ideological and intellectual approaches adopted by the emerging subject of social anthropology and how far these views were incorporated into and defined by the structures and institutions in which they developed. But it is also an analysis of how far the subject was created by its own response to the key issues of the time: colonialism – specifically Africa – anti-Semitism and communism. Goody's approach is characteristically personal: Malinowski dominates the discussion, as well as Fortes, Radcliffe-Brown and Evans-Pritchard, and his own experience, gathered over a varied and wide-ranging life of fieldwork informs the conclusion of the book and the 'whither anthropology?' questions raised by the discussion.

THE EXPANSIVE MOMENT

THE EXPANSIVE MOMENT

MOMENT

The rise of social anthropology
in Britain and Africa 1918–1970

JACK GOODY

University of Cambridge

CAMBRIDGE
UNIVERSITY PRESS

Published by the Press Syndicate of the University of Cambridge
The Pitt Building, Trumpington Street, Cambridge CB2 IRP
40 West 20th Street, New York, NY 10011–4211, USA
10 Stamford Road, Oakleigh, Melbourne 3166, Australia

First published 1995

Printed in Great Britain at the University Press, Cambridge

A catalogue record for this book is available from the British Library

Library of Congress cataloguing in publication data
Goody, Jack.
The expansive moment : the rise of social anthropology in Britain
and Africa, 1918–1970 / Jack Goody.
p.   cm.
Includes bibliographical references.
ISBN 0 521 45048 9 (hardback). – ISBN 0 521 45666 5 (pbk.)
1. Ethnology – Great Britain – History.
2. Ethnology – Africa – History.
I. Title.
GN308.3.G7G66   1995
306'.0941–dc20   94–35663   CIP

ISBN 0 521 45048 9 hardback
ISBN 0 521 45666 5 paperback

CE

Contents

Introduction

Why would one want to read or write a book about a small group of academics, whose fate might interest only practitioners in the same field? Partly because it illustrates the growth and expansion of an area of enquiry and University teaching and research which has had some influence on neighbouring fields. Partly because the accounts which are emerging of that group seem to overlook some crucial aspects of the social and intellectual situation of the 1930s and post-war period. Following an approach current in much intellectual, sociological and cultural history, they assume a homogeneity of interest between intellectuals and the government which neglects internal contradictions and oppositions. Equally intellectual positions were more differentiated, more argued about than such approaches allow, often holding within themselves the clues to the next development. That seems true not only within the group of scholars involved but also of their sponsors, whether these were foundations or governments. In looking at this situation I hope to throw light on the discussion about the relationships of these scholars to the powers that be, which I see as much more differentiated, less homogeneous, than some recent commentators.[1]

As a professional field of enquiry, social anthropology emerged at the beginning of the twentieth century, though it had many earlier progenitors. This book presents an account of the period when this subject came of age in Britain, largely under the auspices of Bronislaw Malinowski, the Polish professor teaching at the London School of Economics (LSE). There he attracted a group of scholars who had already had considerable experience in other fields, who came to form the core around which the major teaching departments in the country were formed, and who founded a tight professional organisation of trained, research-orientated personnel, the Association of Social Anthropologists (ASA), in 1946. Their research consisted mainly of work done in British territories in Africa during the late 1920s and the 1930s, carried out under the auspices of the International African Institute which published much of their results. Although Malinowski was not an Africanist, his personal reputation for fieldwork based on observation and his association with the LSE enabled that Institute to attract money from a philanthropic body in the United States which was interested in the contemporary situation in Africa. This was the Laura Spelman Rockefeller Memorial which contributed significantly to the growth of the social sciences in Britain and had selected the LSE as a centre of excellence worthy of support as early as 1924, at which time it developed a fellowship programme in North America through the newly formed Social Science Research Council (SSRC) – which it had encouraged and financed – as well as in Europe and later Australia.[2]

This then is an account of the interactions of a group of scholars, with many of whom I later worked, and of the research they undertook. Inevitably it concentrates upon my own teachers, Meyer Fortes and E. E. Evans-Pritchard, and in particular on contributions made by research in West Africa where I did my own fieldwork. At the end it becomes frankly autobiographical.

How did I get into this enquiry?

The unfolding of an anthropologist's career, like that of many an academic, can be described in terms of the progression: from the seminar, to the field, to the study and to the class, although one phase does not replace another. One attends seminars as a graduate student and again later on, but in a different capacity and with different intentions, when other professional activities – writing-up or teaching – dominate one's life. For many, probably most, possibly all, academics, writing and teaching themselves gradually take a less important place than administration and politics, that is, than the participation in committees, than the round of learned societies, than the support of one candidate or one issue as against another, and than the multitude of other tasks that tend to overwhelm the pursuits that are normally identified with the profession. Distracting as these are, they form the institutional setting of teaching and research in the context of which takes place a continual hunt for funds and personnel. It is this institutional context of intellectual activity which comes out so clearly in the minutes of meetings and, increasingly over time, in the personal letters of the teachers themselves. It is the relationship between this body of material and their contributions to knowledge in the shape of reviews, papers and books, that lies at the centre of my interest. What I have to offer consists of two parts. The first is an account of the emergence of an academic discipline in this country, largely from the perspective of one of the participants, Meyer Fortes, and to a lesser extent, Evans-Pritchard. The second part is an attempt arising out of an invitation from Claude Tardits to lecture on the subject of 'What did we do?' to a seminar on African anthropology at the 5ème Section de l'Ecole Pratique des Hautes Etudes in Paris in the spring of 1988.

It is often claimed that British social anthropology was the child of colonialism. Its work was carried out mainly within the colonial empire – Malinowski in New Guinea, Radcliffe-Brown in the Andamans, Firth in New Zealand, Tikopia and Malaysia, Evans-Pritchard in the Sudan, Fortes in the Gold Coast, Richards, Gluckman and Schapera in British East and South African territories, Leach in Burma. But the further implication of the claim is that since research had to be carried with the approval and support of these regimes, it influenced both its empirical direction and its theoretical underpinning.[3]

By examining a selection of documents, I want to suggest that these implications need modifying, firstly with regard to the financial base, secondly with regard to the approval of colonial governments, and finally with regard to the supposed homogeneity of the empirical and theoretical approaches. On the individual level, the participants came from differing national, social and ideological backgrounds, though many were influenced by contemporary interests in the ideas of Marx, the rise of Fascism in Europe and the ending of colonial empires. At a social level, the standard claims fail to take account of the contradictions, the conflicts and the diversity of perspective that one finds in any social formation, and specifically in the relations between research worker and the support agencies (whether government or not), and the role of human agency in interpreting, enacting or generating these conflicts. Anthropologists of the 1930s understood this well and they knew, as some have told me, that the situation was yet more complicated than the documents reveal.[4] Nevertheless it seemed to me worthwhile to sketch out the position as it appeared to me from what I had read, even if it confirmed earlier worries about the conclusions one can draw from such textual material.

I have to add that I did not deliberately intend to get involved in this subject at all. In other words, my interest in anthropology has not been in the history of the discipline as such, although I have touched upon the development of some specific intellectual topics. In other words, my interest in history has usually had to do with some problem I was working on, an enterprise in which boundaries have to be breached rather than defined. How then did I come to write these pages?

As a member of the post-war generation of anthropologists, I did not know the two founders of the subject in Britain, A. R. Radcliffe-Brown and B. Malinowski, though I once met the former, and attended his very anthropological funeral; like most funerals of academics, and unlike their weddings and certainly their births, it consisted of colleagues rather than kin. But I did become acquainted with their pupils and colleagues, with Alison Davis, Evans-Pritchard, Firth, Forde, Hogbin, Kaberry, Mair, Mead, Talcott Parsons, Richards, Schapera, Srinivas, Stanner, Lloyd Warner, and with Fortes and Leach I worked closely over many years.

The historical background of social anthropology in early twentieth-century Britain may appear to be a well-worn topic discussed in the works of Jarvie (1964), A. Kuper (1973), Langham (1981), Lombard (1972), Stocking (1983, 1984, 1985) and Kuklick (1991) on the general issues, and of Douglas (1980) on Evans-Pritchard, of Firth (1957) and Panoff (1972) on Malinowski, and of others on particular aspects. I myself took up the topic partly to share the results of some archival research which I undertook when I became interested in a personal file on Fortes in the Ghana archives which related to the difficulties he had in getting to the field and the view taken of his proposal by senior colonial officers; it had been destroyed by the shredders in London, and Fortes told me he did not want to look at it. After his death I was asked to write an extended obituary for the *Proceedings of the British Academy*. I spent some time in the archives of the London School of Economics (before realising that Stocking had looked at many of these) as well as those of the International African Institute since I wanted to produce something substantial, given that these obituaries constitute one of the fullest sources that we have of immediate biographical and bibliographic data, and in some cases of intellectual achievement, especially those on A. R. Radcliffe-Brown and M. Gluckman by R. Firth, C. D. Forde by M. Fortes and E. E. Evans-Pritchard by J. A. Barnes.

For the obituary of Fortes, then, I decided to look at some of the archival materials, including the Public Record Office, and I had access to some of the papers of Meyer Fortes. These pages are a by-product of those enquiries but they originally took shape when I became dissatisfied with some comments on the conservative nature of an undifferentiated British 'structural–functional' anthropology with regard to colonial rule. These came mainly from Americans and Russians whose anthropologists have rarely given much effective support to self-government for the aboriginal peoples of their own immense, internal, empires, contenting themselves with limited ameliorative measures a good deal less radical than those proposed by 'colonial' anthropologists, many of whom supported freedom movements.

But I think of the result as 'notes towards' or a 'personal account' because there are other things I want to write, rather than a full-blown history. Only certain lines are followed up; I am aware there are other documentary sources, close to me, that I have not used. I am also aware of the limitations of the material. While my own background knowledge provides me with anecdotes of the past and residues in the present, I have concentrated upon the documents at my disposal. The results make one realise the limitations of a history based upon written materials, especially letters to close friends. I do not believe one can reconstruct Malinowski's persona from his letters, which express extreme attitudes to Reds and Jews, for example. Yet his behaviour to the outside world regarding Fortes and Kirchhoff, who were both, was exemplary. Equally Evans-Pritchard's letters to Fortes contain the most intolerant, reactionary statements and while he was never a political progressive in any sense, his life was marked by close friendships with two left-leaning Jews. The authors of the letters seem at times to be deliberately striking an extreme attitude as a kind of *épouvantail*, a sick joke, a shocker, to which the other is meant to respond, 'Oh B. M.!', 'Oh E. P.!'

In looking for materials, I have had much help from individuals and institutions, especially the International African Institute. But the attitude of universities and their members towards their own archives worries me. A considerable proportion of their members gain their living by archival research. Through the Public Record Office the Government provides them with excellent facilities to examine most records after a period of thirty years. When I went to the London School of Economics and asked the then Director if I could see the administrative records dating from over fifty years before, I was not allowed direct access, which seems to be one of the perks of the job and provides the basic data for their own histories of the School. I returned to my own university and made a similar request to see the archives, and was told, 'As it is you, there is no problem.' But there is one. Even if universities were not effectively public institutions, they have a collective interest in promoting 'openness', glasnost as we have come to call it, freedom of information. Large numbers of academics live on bits of paper written by other people. There is no excuse for not making records available on the same basis as the government does, that is, thirty years after they have been written, and I hope such access will be a future condition of grants that are made to the universities by the central authorities.

I have wondered about the propriety of using personal correspondence, especially of people I have known, since it seemed like a breach of confidence. Some of this is distasteful enough to lead some readers to want to leave it out. But I have used nothing, except for a few personal observations of my own, that does not appear in a public archive, nothing which is not available, now or in the near future, to other students. So it would be a mistake to bowdlerise their contents by selecting some extracts and deliberately avoiding others, although I do not exclude the possibility of unconscious selection. What I have done is to try and place such remarks in a wider context of understanding, the *verstehen* of the anthropologist. In any case I have not been concerned with aspects of their personal life except in so far as I considered that this affected 'the history of social anthropology'. By this I mean not only the intellectual history but their relations with organisations and colleagues, as these influenced the course of events and the situation in which I and others found ourselves. For in many ways the reader can regard this as 'une recherche du temps perdu'.

I have left untapped a large number of records of this period, partly because they were not always on open shelf, partly because I had limited intentions. But the documents are many. Some have been collected through the efforts of Raymond Firth who in 1974 wrote round to persuade his colleagues of that period to deposit their papers at the London School of Economics. That library contains those of Malinowski, Firth, Richards and Nadel. The Fortes papers are in the University Library at Cambridge. Radcliffe-Brown and Evans-Pritchard appear to have left nothing, or rather to have destroyed all that was in their hands.

CHAPTER I

The economic and organisational basis of British social anthropology in its formative period, 1930–1939: social reform in the colonies

The role of foundations in the social sciences and parallel activities has been the subject of considerable debate. How far were they the tools of capitalism? Were the social policies of the Rockefeller Foundation 'essential cogs in the production and reproduction of cultural hegemony'?[1] The Gramscian argument, espoused by Fisher, places its emphasis on the 'critical-conflict' perspective in the process of knowledge change in which causes are sought in the economy, class, ideology and hegemony. This perspective succeeds in giving to an interesting and informative paper a top-heavy superstructure which does not do justice to the subtlety of the situation, nor yet to Fisher's own analysis. At that level the interpretation has come under attack from Bulmer (1984) and from Karl and Katz (1987). For the attempt to see the social policies as cogs in the reproduction of cultural hegemony overplays the extent of interlocking of family and foundation on the one hand and underestimates the degree of autonomy of structures and actors on the other. As this case history shows there was more conflict, contradiction, disagreement and independence than is often allowed. That conclusion seems even more true of the argument that British social anthropologists as a whole were 'tools of colonialism' since both their interests and those of the foundation that funded them (not to speak of a large part of the British population) rarely coincided with those of colonial governments.

Anthropology, 'the study of man', is a term that goes back to Aristotle and has usually meant the study of the other, the 'primitive' other at that. Its beginnings are lost in the interest that any people has about its neighbours but it emerged as a specific field only in the post-Darwinian era when it was closely associated with the study of the early, undocumented past of mankind (prehistory) and with its physical constitution (physical anthropology, human biology). It became established as a separate field only in the latter part of the century. Sir

Edward Tylor, author of *Primitive Culture* (1871), first lectured in anthropology in Oxford in 1883 when he was appointed keeper of the University Museum. In the following year, the Pitt Rivers Museum was founded and Tylor was made Reader in Anthropology, with responsibility for lecturing on subjects held in the museum. He later became the first Professor of Anthropology in Britain and in 1905 a Diploma in Anthropology was established, the first course offered in a British university. Social anthropology itself was singled out by the appointment of R. R. Marrett as Reader in 1910 and a department was set up in 1914.

The other great name associated with that of Tylor was Sir James Frazer of Cambridge, author of *The Golden Bough* (1892), who was appointed as first Professor of Social Anthropology at Liverpool in 1907 but remained there for only one term. Teaching was developed in Cambridge and London, largely for the purpose of training cadets for the Colonial Service. In 1904 the University of Cambridge established a Board of Anthropological Studies which was to offer teaching in 'prehistoric and historic anthropology, ethnology (including sociology and comparative religion), physical anthropology, and psychological anthropology'.[2] However, a vigorous graduate programme was established only after the First World War under Bronislaw Malinowski at the London School of Economics. That was where most of the action took place during the thirties, not at the ancient universities. His intellectual status, his energy, his enthusiasm and his ability to raise funds resulted in a great expansion of field research. He was able to do this because of his connection with the London School of Economics and through them with the Laura Spelman Rockefeller Memorial which provided the large bulk of the funds.

From the 1930s to the 1960s social anthropology in Britain was marked by a commitment to periods of long and intensive fieldwork, much of it carried out in Africa. Even when the investigator was interested in one aspect more than others, the object was to grasp how social action (behaviour and norms) interacted, how to comprehend the existing community or 'society' as a whole. As such it tended to set aside the comparative and historical dimensions and to focus on the ethnographic present.

That orientation arose partly from a dissatisfaction with the results of earlier anthropology, which was now seen as engaging in doubtful reconstructions of the past and in the global comparison based upon inadequate ethnographic fieldwork. But it also coincided with a massive increase of funding that enabled research workers to be trained and to make intensive enquiries, as well as the arrival on the scene of highly motivated scholars. Under the inspiration of the Polish anthropologist, Bronislaw Malinowski, they formed a small group that experienced the usual friendships and enmities, but which on the intellectual level gave consideration to a number of related problems which they managed to advance and clarify by reference to field observations and to social theory.

On a theoretical level their orientation turned around the notion of 'functionalism' which some rejected or modified in favour of a more 'structural' approach. Both those approaches had their origin in the work of nineteenth-century reformers, Comte and Spencer and above all in that of the French socialist thinker, Emile Durkheim. Radcliffe-Brown had lectured on sociology in Cambridge in 1908 (as the classicist Jane Harrison attests); Malinowski encouraged his graduate students to read *Année sociologique*.[3] That influence represented the important shift in British anthropology. But these new anthropologists were more concerned with concrete problems of matrilineal systems, lineage organisation, the developmental cycle, witchcraft, the nature and settlement of disputes and so forth. Current American interpretations of the development of anthropology sometimes find this approach consistent with the interests of colonial authorities, of whom the anthropologists were their pensioners if not their prisoners, even their unconscious mouthpieces. My reading of the evidence derived from archives and from personal contacts suggests that such a view needs to be heavily qualified. Firstly it neglects the motivation, origin and background of most anthropologists (many from overseas), as well as the leftward, sometimes Marxist, leanings of university life at that time, especially at the London School of Economics where Malinowski taught. Secondly, it overlooks the fact that the major source of funding lay in an American foundation with reformist rather than imperial interests. Thirdly, these two factors heightened the suspicions of administrators in the colonies towards academic research, even if those in London were more open to enquiry in the social sciences.

In the period after the Second World War, the sources of funds shifted and much research was then undertaken under the auspices of the newly founded Colonial Social Science Research Council, at a period when India and Burma had already achieved independence and when that goal had appeared on the horizon of colonial dependencies throughout the world, in other words in the twilight of colonial rule.

The funds were distributed by a body consisting largely of academics who were under little or no pressure from the authorities, according to priorities sketched out in the reports of senior anthropologists. The recipients of the grants included students from the USA, the Indian subcontinent, from China as well as from Britain and other Commonwealth countries. The subsequent spread of the teaching of anthropology in universities gradually weakened the small-group atmosphere generated by these scholars, who had spent their earlier years in research rather than in undergraduate teaching. A diversity of interests in more historical and comparative topics (including the comparative, symbolic studies of Lévi-Strauss) began to manifest themselves. New perspectives were opened up in the work of those who constituted the third and fourth generations. But at the same time something was lost when the field became so diffuse, when the audience consisted of undergraduates rather than colleagues, when the focus on common problems (as distinct from philosophical trends) tended to disappear. That is the background to the story I present in the chapters that follow. My account dwells primarily on Africa. That is not simply the result of a personal quirk: it was the continent where the bulk of the research took place, partly because of the earlier grants by the Rockefeller philanthropies to the International African Institute and the later ones by the Colonial Social Science Research Council. If I concentrate unashamedly on work in that continent, I do not mean to underrate the importance of the research carried out in India (especially by M. N. Srinivas), in Burma (by E. R. Leach), in the Pacific (by Firth, Fortune and others) and in other parts of the globe by anthropologists associated with the British 'school'.

The development of social anthropology in Britain obviously had much to do with the position of the country as a colonial power, as was the case in Russia, in the USA and in France. In that country professional field research was of little significance until the thirties when funds became available to train and finance anthropologists. But those funds came largely from outside, as did the anthropologists themselves. Neither the givers nor the bulk of the recipients were primarily interested in propping up colonial empires. For Africa, the Colonial Office was concerned with the problems of ruling a large empire. While, unlike India, the movement to independence in that continent did not achieve much momentum until after the Second World War, with its promises of a new dispensation, many politicians, backed by a significant segment of the population, were interested not only in reform but in a gradual movement towards independence. It was with the more extreme of these elements that most anthropologists in Britain were identified.

At that time the main impetus, or at least the means, for the growth of fieldwork and of the subject more generally was dependent on the activities of the Laura Spelman Rockefeller Memorial set up in 1918 in memory of the wife of John D. Rockefeller, Snr. The Memorial was established partly to take care of 'the more dangerous social concerns' which had been excluded from the scope of the Rockefeller Foundation ever since the McKenzie King affair of 1914–15 when it had been heavily criticised for mixing research and business interests. Some seven years later Beardsley Ruml, who had taken a doctorate in psychology at Chicago, was appointed Director.[4] That appointment represented a change from social welfare to social science and public administration, as well as to professional specialisation among foundation staff. Within two years he had transformed 'an unremarkable charity into a major vehicle for funding basic social science', much of it in Britain.[5] Social studies were to be converted to academic social science.

The Memorial was one of four groups sharing in the 450 million dollars accumulated by the founder, which in 1928 became the Division of Social Sciences in the Rockefeller Foundation. During the course of the 1920s the Memorial broadened its aims to comprise support of higher learning, including overseas, and to promote human welfare. The profound importance of this relatively small foundation for the development of American social science has been examined by Martin Bulmer and others;[6] it had a similar influence in Britain and other parts of the English-speaking world.

The social sciences were not the only academic field in Britain to gain from the largesse of the Rockefeller philanthropies. The Rockefeller Foundation played a major role in the development of 'scientific medicine' in this country, that is, in the integration of medical schools, hospitals and universities, in the encouragement of units in research and teaching and in the establishment of chairs in specialist fields.[7] These enormous benefactions, especially to the London School of Hygiene and Tropical Medicine and to University College, were made under a policy developed by Wickliffe Rose who administered the projects in the medical field and who had decided that the best way to develop a field of knowledge was to identify and strengthen centres of excellence, providing fellowships to bring other scholars to study there.[8] Fellowship programmes attached to these centres were key developments in academic philanthropy in America following the First World War.

Initially established to support the kind of social welfare projects in which Mrs Rockefeller had been personally interested, the Memorial was reoriented towards the social sciences when Beardsley Ruml was appointed director in 1922. Ruml had been a graduate student in psychology at Chicago between 1915 and 1917 where the social sciences had already become well established under the sociologists W. I. Thomas, Robert Park (after 1914) and Albion W. Small; it was Small's vision of 'group study as opposed to departmental study or individual study', elaborated in conjunction with the political scientist, Charles Merriam, and the economist, Leon Marshall, that stimulated Ruml's policy for the Foundation. Within a year or so of his appointment he approached the trustees with a view to investing in the social sciences (which meant 'sociology, ethnology, anthropology and psychology, and certain aspects of economics, history, political economy and biology') in order to provide a scientific basis for social welfare.

In the following year, 1923, the three Chicago departments of political science, of sociology and anthropology, and of political economy presented to the trustees of the Foundation a plan which aimed to make fundamental contributions to the methods and achievements of the social sciences through a study of the problems of the local community. Approval of the plan meant that Park, Burgess and their associates could undertake 'maps of urban growth, through the mapping of local community areas, studies of the distribution of juvenile delinquency, juvenile gangs, family disorganisation and divorce, and detailed investigations of homeless men, hotel life, rooming-house keepers and the Lower North Side', as well as a great deal of other work. The resulting publications included those minor classics, Thrasher's *The Gang*, Zorbaugh's *Gold Coast and the Slum*, Cressey's *Taxi Dance Hall* and Louis Wirth's *The Ghetto*.

Under the stimulation of Ruml the philanthropy of the Memorial was not limited to Chicago, nor yet to the United States. Together with his friend Merriam, Ruml encouraged the founding of the Social Science Research Council in America. While through Rockefeller largesse this body awarded fellowships rather than grants, it became a kind of forerunner for such councils in other parts of the world. In England the first such body was significantly the Colonial Social Science Research Council, founded in 1944 under the enlightened secretaryship of Sally Chilver; the Social Science Research Council was only established by the Labour Government in 1965 under the Directorship of Michael (now Lord) Young, and in 1984 its name was changed under direct pressure from the Conservative government to the Economic and Social Research Council – the only one in the English-speaking world to exclude the phrase 'social science'.[9] One of Ruml's first moves as Director of the Memorial was to commission a report on the social sciences in America by L. K. Frank, which concluded that very few enquiries employed 'scientific research involving actual experimentation and investigation' and that there was barely any provision 'for training in scientific methods'.[10] Between 1923 and 1929, when the Memorial became part of the main Rockefeller Foundation, Ruml distributed $21 million for fundamental work in the social sciences. In Britain the main beneficiary was the London School of Economics which under Beveridge's direction received $2 million between 1923 and 1939.[11] Beveridge and Ruml had met in September 1923 and got on well together. Both agreed that the social sciences were too abstract and required more emphasis on empirical observation. As a result of their discussions the School became one of the five major beneficiaries of the Foundation's generosity, which financed the Library, buildings, professorships, research projects and visits to the United States.[12] It was under these auspices that the dynamic Professor of Anthropology at the School, Bronislaw Malinowski, was invited to visit America at the same time as Radcliffe-Brown who was about to move from Cape Town to Sydney to take up the Chair in Anthropology founded in 1926 with Rockefeller support. Malinowski too established friendly relations with the Foundation personnel and approached them independently for help. For example, he appealed to them in 1930 when the Sydney Chair in Anthropology seemed to be threatened by Radcliffe-Brown's impending departure for Chicago and the possible withdrawal of national funds; Malinowski was keen to see that chair filled by a former student, Raymond Firth, who later succeeded him at the London School of Economics.[13] But his major contribution in attracting funds was to that School and to the newly formed International African Institute.

The London School of Economics was already central in the institutional development of British social anthropology. Although the first full-time appointment was not made there until 1913, a course in 'ethnology' had been given in 1904–5 by A. C. Haddon of Cambridge, and was thought likely to interest 'civil servants destined for the tropical portions of the empire' together with missionaries.[14] A similar development took place in Cambridge, beginning in 1906 with instruction arranged for prospective Indian civil servants and in 1908 for those going to work in the Sudan. In his London teaching, Haddon was followed by Radcliffe-Brown who had been elected to a fellowship at Trinity College, Cambridge, on his return from the Andaman Islands. Charles Seligman, a medical doctor who had accompanied the Torres Straits expedition – one of the first attempts at professional anthropological research in Britain, organised by A. C. Haddon, originally a zoologist – succeeded him in 1910 and he received a permanent appointment in 1913 as part-time Professor of Anthropology. In May 1923 Malinowski, who had been giving lectures there since his return from the Trobriands, was elected Reader in Social Anthropology, a title which he himself had suggested, partly to distinguish the School from University College where proposals had been made for a Readership in Cultural Anthropology, and partly because ' "social" will also indicate that our interest is mainly sociological'.[15] That post itself was made possible by the Rockefeller funding.

Cambridge also acquired a Readership (in Ethnology) when A. C. Haddon was appointed in 1909 – he had been made a lecturer in 1900; but there was no Chair until the William Wyse Professorship was established in 1932 by a friend of J. G. Frazer and filled first by T. C. Hodson, then by J. H. Hutton (both formerly of the Indian Civil Service) and then by a student of Malinowski, Meyer Fortes. The Chair in Social Anthropology at Oxford (Tylor had previously held a professorship in general anthropology) was initially held by Radcliffe-Brown from 1937 until he retired in 1946, again to be followed by another student from the London School, E. E. Evans-Pritchard. Radcliffe-Brown had previously held the first Chair of Social Anthropology in Cape Town in 1921, and five years later he moved to Sydney which with the help of Rockefeller money he made the base for research personnel from America and Great Britain who were working in Australia and the Pacific. In addition he founded the journal *Oceania*.[16] It was not accidental that he moved from Sydney to Chicago, the cradle of Rockefeller generosity to the social sciences (where he was pushed partly because of the threat to funds) nor that the move should lead Malinowski to worry about the influence he might wield in those quarters where he was so well placed. However, in Sydney it was a pupil of Malinowski, Raymond Firth, who took over his responsibilities (but not his Chair).

It was at the London School of Economics, in the late twenties, that Malinowski proclaimed anthropology in Britain, his anthropology, to be the one kind that mattered. That anthropology was based on extensive fieldwork, preferably with one tribe or people, and in this he saw the key to the development of the social sciences and to their contribution to practical life. Indeed it was his success in convincing the Rockefeller philanthropies of the value of his approach that was an important constituent in the opening up of anthropological research in Britain. Before that its history had been essentially linear, a pedigree rather than a branching genealogy, a descent line rather than a ramifying lineage. One man handed over to the next. Even Malinowski's pupils were few and far between in the twenties. He started his famous seminar soon after he took up his appointment as Reader in 1923. At first it consisted of Evans-Pritchard (who had studied history at Oxford), of Ashley Montague (whose main work was on the biological side), of Ursula Grant-Duff (the daughter of Lord Avebury, an important figure in the earlier history of British anthropology), of Raymond Firth (who had studied economics in New Zealand), and of Barbara Freire-Marresco (or Mrs Aitken, who worked among the Tewa of Hano in the south-west of the USA). When Hortense Powdermaker, a trade-union organiser from America, arrived there in 1925 and eventually wrote a study of Hollywood as well as of the Copper Belt of Zambia, there were only three graduate students in anthropology: she herself, Evans-Pritchard and Firth, followed the next year by Isaac Schapera who had worked under Radcliffe-Brown at Cape Town. As we have seen, Evans-Pritchard, who did fieldwork among the Nuer and the Azande of the Sudan, was to fill the Chair at Oxford. Firth carried out research among the Maori (before going to London), in Malaya and above all on the Pacific island of Tikopia, prior to becoming the successor to Malinowski in London. Schapera worked extensively among the black population of Southern Africa and he too became a professor at the School. However, Powdermaker was soon joined by others who were to become well-known in British anthropology, Audrey Richards, a natural scientist from Cambridge who was to work among the Bemba of Zambia, Edith Clarke from Jamaica, and by Jack Driberg (a former colonial officer), Camilla Wedgwood, and Gordon and Elizabeth Brown of Canada, who carried out fieldwork in East Africa, Melanesia and East Africa respectively.

Several of these students were in receipt of grants or fellowships from the Rockefeller Memorial, which in 1929 had opened the way for anthropologists to apply. Clarke, Mair and Richards fall into this category. But the great development came with the establishment of the Fellowship programme of the International African Institute in 1931, a programme that was also called upon to provide grants for Richards, the Browns and Clarke, though never for Evans-Pritchard or Driberg, who by that time had come to oppose Malinowski, an opposition that led the former to seek a strong link with Radcliffe-Brown.

Of course, the Rockefeller Memorial was not the only source of funds for anthropological research. Malinowski himself had received a grant to work in New Guinea from Dr Robert Mond; Gregory Bateson was supported for his enquiries in New Guinea by a Research Fellowship at St John's College, Cambridge, as well as by other grants; Edmund Leach carried out his initial work among the Kurds using his own funds; during the war Firth was supported in Malaysia by a grant from the Leverhulme Foundation; Radcliffe-Brown held an Anthony Wilkin Studentship from Cambridge; for his work among the Azande Evans-Pritchard obtained grants from the Royal Society and the Government of the Sudan. Nevertheless, Rockefeller money made grants available through the Australian National Research Council (of which Radcliffe-Brown and later Firth were secretaries of the relevant committee) as well as through the International African Institute. Meanwhile the British government did very little. Although the Universities of Oxford, Cambridge and London produced and to some extent trained most of the personnel that staffed the colonies, which (as in Paris) was a major part of the justification for teaching the subject of anthropology at those institutions, very little money was provided for ethnographic research. It is true that there were some government anthropologists in the colonial service: Rattray in Ghana (Gold Coast) and Meek in Nigeria. They were men who had started their careers as administrators and then had become involved in studying the lives of the people.[17] Apart from the awards to Seligman and later to Evans-Pritchard from the government of the Anglo-Egyptian Sudan, there was little support for outside ethnographic research in British territories. Even in India, where much work was done, it was largely carried out by administrative officers.[18] Nor did missionary societies make much contribution outside their own ranks, while the great capitalist concerns that were making money out of Africa were equally sparing of their finances. Although each of these interests was represented on the Executive Committee of the International African

Institute, its research funds came not from Britain at all but from America. Anthropology on the continent of Europe had a yet harder struggle for independent funds and one recalls the great efforts Griaule had to undertake in France, putting on a circus, promoting fights, in order to raise funds for his expeditions.

By 1937 the situation in British Africa had begun to change with the establishment of the Rhodes–Livingstone Institute in Northern Rhodesia (Zambia) with the aid of government and private contributions.[19] Nevertheless the Rockefeller philanthropies played the dominant part in financing research. The greater largesse of America was partly due to the huge accumulations of the early 'robber barons', partly to the nature of tax laws and partly to the higher propensity for charitable giving; indeed the three are very closely intertwined. As a result of this generosity, anthropologists could look forward to several years on a well-financed grant to carry out research, which was undoubtedly a factor in attracting senior research workers to come and join with Malinowski in London.

The inauguration of the International African Institute had followed from a meeting at the School of Oriental Studies in September 1925 (before 'African' had been added to the title of that School) as the result of a series of consultations among academic, missionary, educational and administrative interests. It was founded the following year with the help of a grant of £1,000 a year for five years from the Laura Spelman Rockefeller Memorial. Towards the end of that period the Institute thought of applying for additional funds, but it was intimated to them that the Rockefeller Foundation, whose Social Science Division the Memorial had now become, considered that there was too much administration and not enough research. A substantial programme was then submitted to the Foundation for Fellowships and grants. As a result the Institute received an award of £10,000 a year for five years from 1931 and established a special bureau to deal with these matters.

The key figure behind the new Institute was Dr J. H. Oldham, a missionary, educationalist and administrator who was committed to the acquisition and diffusion of scientific knowledge (in the widest sense) about Africa with a view to social amelioration. Oldham, once described as 'that arch intriguer for good', had been involved as early as 1912 in the attempt to apply the Tuskegee policy concerning the non-academic training of southern American Negroes to the continent of Africa. From 1908 to 1910 he had been secretary of the World

Missionary Conference at Edinburgh and from 1910 to 1921 he was secretary of its Continuation Committee. Besides being secretary of the International Missionary Council he also edited the *International Review of Missions* which became 'the quasi-official journal of the Protestant missionary societies in Great Britain from its inception in 1912'.[20]

Oldham was a key figure in the group searching for elements of a uniform educational policy for Africa and in 1923 was associated with the founding of the British Advisory Committee on Native Education in Tropical Africa, which adopted the Tuskegee policy emphasising vocational rather than literary education, described by a critic as 'the surest way to achieve the formation of a malleable and docile African worker'.[21] It was in this context that Hanns Vischer, the chairman of the Committee, an ex-colonial officer and later secretary of the International African Institute, was sent on a three-week study tour of the American South.

This enterprise had already received assistance from the Laura Spelman Rockefeller Memorial which became the main support of the International African Institute. But the aims were obviously very different. Moreover the criticisms levelled at the attempt to make African education more sensitive to rural life are partly misdirected. It was not a choice between agricultural and literary education with the aim of excluding the African from the latter. The missionary societies set up many secondary schools along British lines which were directed towards the academic side and which achieved some remarkable results. But anyone who has sat through watered-down versions of a similar curriculum in a rural African school, most of whose pupils will have to return to agriculture for decades to come (and hoe agriculture at that), must wonder about the appropriateness of much that was included from European urban models. In any case academic and practical courses are not alternative paths but complementary ones, whose nature and mix must be related to the society at large. Certainly in West Africa secondary and higher education made great strides, though this has often been more in the individual's than in the nation's interest, since it has provided students with the ability to sell their labour abroad for higher rewards than the country itself can afford. The argument is much more shaded than has been allowed but certainly, like most missionaries, Oldham's interest in African education was not confined to the encouragement of the practical. The International African Institute, for example, was devoted to the cultural and to research.

Oldham and Malinowski became close friends and developed an intimate working relationship, with Malinowski often complaining about the way things were going (usually with humour) and Oldham replying in a soothing, diplomatic tone and always depending upon his friend's academic judgement, to the exclusion, it should be said, of other voices such as those of the Directors from the Continent, the linguist and ethnologist Diedrich Westermann of Germany and the administrator and ethnologist Henri Labouret of France, as well as of other council members such as Seligman who had considerable African experience. Seligman, who was Malinowski's fellow Professor at the London School of Economics, had not only been a member of A. C. Haddon's expedition to the Torres Straits in 1898, but had also carried out work in the Anglo-Egyptian Sudan and it was under his supervision that Evans-Pritchard was working.

Plans for the Fellowship scheme began to crystallise in the latter part of 1930. In September of that year Malinowski wrote to Oldham from his Italian home reporting on a meeting with Van Sickle, Paris representative of the Rockefeller Foundation, referring to 'our plan' and to 'the London group'.[22] Oldham replied congratulating Malinowski: 'If this venture meets with success it will owe more to you than to anybody else.'[23] Earlier that year he had thanked Malinowski for agreeing to act as secretary to the group, remarking that this was especially important because of Seligman, who was at once an Africanist and a representative of the Royal Anthropological Institute on the Council. Malinowski was determined to set aside any influence he had, regarding him as an antiquarian ethnologist.

So Malinowski's influence was dominant. In June 1931 Hanns Vischer, the ex-colonial officer who was Secretary-General of the Institute, wrote thanking him for the help he had given Oldham in preparing the Rockefeller proposal, and declaring that 'anthropology for us is social anthropology after the manner in which you teach it'.[24] No wonder then that Malinowski, who became the holder of a Chair specifically entitled Social Anthropology (as Frazer's had been in Liverpool), found it difficult to get on with his former patron, Seligman, the part-time Professor of Ethnology. For he needed to be alone in charge, the sole prophet of the new science of man. Malinowski admitted to a 'one-sided sociological interest', a development that Seligman opposed.[25] Indeed he complained to Oldham that Seligman had attacked him at the University Board of Studies, insisting that students who wanted to study social anthropology should also work on prehistory, physical anthropology, archaeology and the distribution of man, the whole range of the post-Darwinian field of studies.[26]

How was it that Malinowski achieved this dominant position in the African Institute when he had done no work in that continent? As early as 1927 Oldham wrote to Malinowski about the latter's approaches to Rockefeller, and in 1929 he visited the USA and entered into negotiations with the Foundation.[27] Some twenty-seven months later their correspondence contained a specific reference to the fact that Malinowski had approached Ruml and his deputy (and successor as head of the Social Science Division from 1929), Dean Day, about the Institute.[28] A few days later Malinowski sent Day a memorandum about the possibility of research in Africa, following up discussions they had had in the spring of 1929. He pointed out the parallel to the Foundation's existing work in the Pacific, carried out under the supervision of Radcliffe-Brown, and reminded him that in Autumn 1929 the Foundation had extended its Fellowship scheme, first intended to bring young scholars to the United States, to include the possibility of anthropological fieldwork.[29]

The incorporation of the Laura Spelman Memorial into the main Rockefeller foundation in 1929 had shifted the focus of its support from academic institutions to the 'promotion of the welfare of mankind and not for scattered projects in basic science'.[30] Support grew for the anthropology of the contemporary world. As Head of the Social Science Division, Day became fed up with what he saw as the lack of co-operation from anthropologists in the States, and this perception inclined him to look to the Institute for scientific co-operation.[31] This was not only a personal matter, but rather a positive attraction to Malinowski's 'functional' anthropology in contrast to the antiquarian studies prevalent elsewhere, combined with the prospect of the access to Africa that the Institute could provide through its relation with the colonial authorities. The terms are Malinowski's, but it is clear that he convinced the social scientists manning the Rockefeller Foundation whose intellectual and practical predilections already leant towards a sociological approach. Functionalism and fieldwork meant an interest in the functioning rather than the historical, the quick rather than the dead, the present rather than the past. The Foundation was interested in what was happening now, in what could be learned by observation in actual situations, in the kind of fieldworking functionalism that Malinowski was advocating.

The memorandum on policy, which was to form the basis of the research programme of the Institute, was drafted by the Directors in September 1931, the major part being played by Oldham who was the Administrative Director. Westermann's contribution was entirely rewritten by Audrey Richards, who consulted Malinowski by letter at every stage, for he remained at his Italian home until the 10th Executive Council meeting of the Institute, held in Paris on 14 and 15 October of that year.

At the time the policy document was being prepared, Radcliffe-Brown was in England and was consulted by Oldham who duly reported to Malinowski that 'Radcliffe-Brown has come on the scene and will be an important factor.'[32] Malinowski's views were clear cut. While he respected Radcliffe-Brown's work, he did not want anything to do with him personally. At first he remained silent; 'On Radcliffe-Brown I shall say nothing.'[33] But three months later he wrote from Toulon, saying, 'if Radcliffe-Brown got into England, it would be a damn bad job for our Institute as well as for everybody else'. The struggle for the control of resources was clear to one and all.[34]

When the memorandum for the research grant to be submitted to the Rockefeller Foundation had been prepared, it was then submitted to Radcliffe-Brown and Malinowski for comments. Their reactions were different. On the contents of the policy document Radcliffe-Brown commented, firstly, that it should have more focus, and secondly, that it should avoid involving anthropologists in value judgements about policy.[35] He wrote:

I think it would be better if the Institute's investigations all dealt with the subject in a purely scientific way, confining themselves to the precise observation of what is taking place and not concerning themselves with what is good and bad in the original society or in the changes that it is undergoing, nor with the practical problems. The task of the investigator should be to obtain exact knowledge, impartially presented, in such a form that it can be immediately utilised by those who are actually concerned with native government and education.[36]

For Malinowski, the first suggestion ran contrary to the particular holistic approach he espoused, while the second was incompatible with his practical orientation. He replied, saying: 'There is no doubt we are all aiming at the same thing, that is, a thoroughgoing study of several tribes from the point of view of contact with European culture, the ensuing changes and the possibilities of controlling these changes.'[37] That was Rockefeller's aim. While he agreed with Radcliffe-Brown's substantive comments he could not accept his view about the study of

social change. He remarked that: 'I think the Institute's investigators
should be as fully aware of practical problems and of the "good" and
"bad" in the original society and in the changes, as is possible.' In a
letter written on the following day he recommends the work of Audrey
Richards who, with Gordon-Brown, is 'the best of my Lieutenants',
since she has shown how to do 'practical anthropology in the field'.
The emphasis on practicality seemed to be encouraged by the known
interests of the Foundation. At this point the funds were calling at least
part of the tune.

The fact that Malinowski was living at such a distance from London
meant that he could not exercise any direct control over the text, but
his students on the drafting committee regularly reported back to him,
as did Dorothy Brackett (the Administrative Secretary), Oldham and
Westermann. Immediately after the meeting of that committee
Richards sent him an account which revealed the full extent of the split
that had already developed in social anthropology in Britain. She
explained that while 'the FAITHFUL have the field to themselves',
during the course of the discussion she came to realise that a larger
plan was at stake. 'Gordon and I immediately guessed at Radcliffe-
Brown's snaffling up the anthropological part of this sum in his
American trip' if the Institute's policy is not formed straight away. She
hoped his advice will not be taken 'on general principles' (though it is
largely in agreement with Malinowski's) and 'hearing that E.-P. is
making up to him' (R.-B.), began to see possibilities of future strife.[38]
While the composition of the 'faithful' was not absolutely fixed and
while there were important cross-cutting ties, the expression was used
by those both in and out of the group.[39] Radcliffe-Brown certainly
constituted a bogeyman for Malinowski too, for about the same time
he wrote to Hall at the Rockefeller Foundation of a meeting which was
'mainly about future anthropology plans, above all about a man
named Radcliffe-Brown, who wants to open a big anthropological
centre at the School of Oriental Studies', which was one of the rival
possibilities.[40]

Evans-Pritchard had already crossed swords with Malinowski as
early as 1925. The latter had suggested to Firth that he come to
London from Sydney, where he had succeeded Radcliffe-Brown as
acting head, to take up the position of director of the research
programme of the International African Institute.[41] 'Naturally',
remarked Malinowski, 'I hope to retain my influence.' When this
appointment proved impossible because of Firth's lack of African

experience, he wrote again urging him to apply for a Fellowship. About other possible applicants he was less keen:

as to the claims of such people as J. H. Driberg and E. Evans-Pritchard, both of them are not very popular with anybody who knows them, and it would be quite useless for me to try pushing them into any position which requires loyalty and decent cooperation with other people . . . As to Evans-Pritchard, I have definitely stipulated to Seligman, that if Evans-Pritchard gets a permanent post at the L.S.E., I would write tendering my resignation.

The particular complaint that occasioned this comment appeared to be that Driberg, with Evans-Pritchard's knowledge, had corresponded with one Rentoul of Papua (now Papua-New Guinea) behind Malinowski's back, in order to be able to query his statements about the Trobrianders' lack of knowledge of a connection between intercourse and procreation. Rentoul was a magistrate who served on the Trobriands after Malinowski's day.

Later that year, on hearing that Evans-Pritchard and Driberg were to be encouraged to work 'really hard for the Institute' (like Malinowski himself, who had done so 'in an entirely disinterested way'), Malinowski remarked: 'The real trouble about some of our younger colleagues is that . . . they are incapable of honest and disinterested service.'[42] Richards spoke in even stronger terms, telling Malinowski in September that she had written 'a gloomy letter to Elsie [her sister] about the whole crew', but cheered up on realising that 'E.-P. can't speak about anyone without sneering, friend or foe alike'. At this point she had recently been to hear Radcliffe-Brown give a talk in London on education in Melanesia, the content of which she approved. Indeed Radcliffe-Brown himself made a favourable impression, and Richards wrote to Malinowski that he 'himself was quite decent about your work – merely disagreed with it, and thought himself the more eminent of the two! Which is just what we think of his work.'[43]

The conflict over the policy document is interesting for a number of wider issues. One aspect of ideas, especially in the less obviously accumulating fields of knowledge, is their role in relating people one to another. From this standpoint Malinowski and Radcliffe-Brown are often linked together in the so-called structural-functional school. The term was not Malinowski's, for he insisted on a 'functional' approach, and saw Radcliffe-Brown as part of the same school, though an erratic member who had more links with antiquarian predecessors. With his interest in Spencer (as well of course as in Durkheim), Radcliffe-Brown was more concerned to lay emphasis on 'structure', and it was in the emphasis on this concept (or rather on 'social structure') that the group of people with whom he later worked at Oxford distinguished themselves.

The intellectual character of the discrepancies between Malinowski and Radcliffe-Brown seems of a fairly minor kind compared with their convergences, and compared with the alternative trends in American and European anthropology at the time. When Radcliffe-Brown left Sydney in 1931 he wrote a very friendly letter to Malinowski, speaking of 'our common aim'.[44] In the previous October Malinowski had written to the Rockefeller Foundation saying that Radcliffe-Brown was 'one of the best anthropologists and also an excellent organiser', although adding that he could not get on with the university.[45] The difficulties between them arose partly out of the dominant role played by Malinowski in Britain and the concurrent attempt of some of his students to align themselves with an alternative focus of academic power and intellectual achievement. Thus the constellation, Seligman, Evans-Pritchard, Radcliffe-Brown, became somewhat opposed to that of Malinowski, Richards and in a sense Firth, though cross-cutting ties were always present. Intellectually the work of Evans-Pritchard was certainly closer to the sociological approach of the Malinowski group than to the eclecticism of Seligman. Firth in particular had close relations with Evans-Pritchard, though the latter was often critical of his attitudes towards authority; Evans-Pritchard's close friend and colleague, Meyer Fortes, probably had more respect for Firth's work than did his colleague, as he had for that of Nadel and Forde. Nevertheless an opposition existed and an appreciation of it is significant for the intellectual history of anthropologists like Fortes whose ties of friendship were with Evans-Pritchard but whose financial resources depended upon Malinowski. Moreover, it also had something to do with the different emphasis of teaching at the two most important formative departments in Britain in the early fifties, the London School of Economics and Oxford, as well as with the growing strength of Cambridge in the later part of the decade. Here I want to emphasise neither the priority of the intellectual dispute, nor the intellectual consequences of the opposition, but rather the organisational aspects of the quarrel.

The divergence between these two groups had a history going back to the 1920s. At the London School of Economics Malinowski had to work with Seligman, the supervisor of Evans-Pritchard's work in

Africa, but his correspondence in the early thirties displays some hostility towards Seligman, more towards Radcliffe-Brown and most of all towards Evans-Pritchard. The split took a territorial form with separate High Courts being held in summer at Seligman's home at Toot Baldon and at Malinowski's residence at Sopra Bolzano, to which their respective friends were invited. One can exaggerate the division. For Evans-Pritchard and Schapera stayed at Bolzano, while Firth and Richards went to Toot Baldon. There was also of course interchange on the intellectual level. Gluckman attended Malinowski's seminars while Firth went to stay with Radcliffe-Brown and Evans-Pritchard at All Souls, Oxford. Firth remarks that 'despite the intellectual differences which separated Seligman from Malinowski in later years over general versus social anthropology, there was much coming and going between them'.[46] Nevertheless a cleavage existed and one continuing focus was the struggle for resources.

Both Malinowski and Radcliffe-Brown received strong support from the Rockefeller Foundation. But an element in the opposition between the two was control of posts, students and monetary grants. While at Sydney Radcliffe-Brown built up anthropological research in the Pacific, and at Chicago, in the Americas, largely on Rockefeller money; Malinowski was to do the same at the London School of Economics for Africa, a continent in which he had no personal experience before making an extended trip at the Foundation's expense. I do not wish to imply that there was no theoretical basis for the opposition between the two men and their respective 'adherents', although that has been much exaggerated. But institutional affiliation (which creates or imposes its own loyalties, though in no automatic fashion) and conflicts over resources were factors of considerable importance in any intellectual history – or rather history of intellectuals – that looks at the development of British social anthropology. At the same time there were a number of cross-cutting ties, especially among their students. What is remarkable is the degree of coherence at the level of professional activity and approach to the subject of those trained by Malinowski and Radcliffe-Brown. That was the great strength of the subject at the time.

CHAPTER 2

Training for the field: the sorcerer's apprentices

Once the Rockefeller Foundation had agreed to sponsor the Fellowship scheme, which started in July 1931, the Institute had to look round for possible recipients. It was here that Malinowski exercised his patronage and made his influence felt. While he had at first no official position with the Institute, his relations with the Foundation, his friendship with Oldham, the missionary administrator of the scheme, and his participation in meetings of the Africa group, which brought him into contact with the influential colonial administrator, Lord Lugard, and others, made his co-operation essential for the fulfilment of the programme, including the training of the participants.

In recruiting Fellows Malinowski naturally thought first of his own students, while the Directors of the Institute also played a part. But it was the Bureau, formed to administer the grants, that carried out the interviews and made recommendations to the Council of the Institute. The initial selection included a number of people with whom Malinowski had worked and approved of. 'What then with Gordon Brown, Fortes, Audrey Richards, Margery Perham and Kirchkoff [*sic*], we have got quite a good set of young people.'[1] Additional Rockefeller Fellowships had been previously awarded to Lucy Mair, who was Lecturer in Colonial Administration (and whose mother was secretary of the School, under the Director, Beveridge) and Edith Clarke, a well-connected student of Jamaican background, who was about to go to the Gold Coast. All except Kirchhoff, who had already been employed by Rockefeller and was recommended by Westermann, Director of the Institute, were 'students' of Malinowski, though Gordon Brown was at Toronto, Audrey Richards teaching and Fortes had not yet studied anthropology.

The Fellows later appointed by the Institute were drawn from a much wider range and made up a remarkable collection. So many foreigners were included in the first Fellowships that Kitteridge expressed the hope that 'you will have enough English students to balance the group'.[2] Although many of them had little previous experience of anthropology they were to form much of the core of the teaching of African studies for the next thirty and more years. The seventeen full-time Fellows were Fortes (South Africa), Hofstra (Holland), Kirchhoff (Germany), Nadel (Austria), together with the two Kriges (South Africa), Lucy Mair (Britain), Margery Perham (Britain), Margaret Read (Britain), Monica Wilson (Britain), Matthews (a Masuto), another German, G. K. Wagner, another Austrian, the missionary, Father Schumacher (who worked in Ruanda), two French-women, T. Rivière, the niece of G. H. Rivière, and Germaine Tillion, who worked in North Africa and was later interned in a concentration camp, and two linguists, Father Crazzolora (Italy) and J. Lukas (Germany).[3] Grants were made, among others, to Jomo Kenyatta of Kenya (later the leader of the independence struggle) and to Fadipe from Yorubaland, so that they could work at the London School of Economics. Indeed a number of the other Fellows were asked to come to London to work under Malinowski. As a result of his endeavours, the Institute, combined with the London School of Economics, became 'a factory of really competent anthropologists and sociologists'.[4] The list of students attending Malinowski's seminars at the School in the session 1932–3 consisted mainly of Africanists, all of whom produced valuable studies: H. Beemer (later Kuper), M. Fortes, M. Lecoeur, S. F. Nadel, S. Hofstra, M. Read, G. Wilson, M. Perham, L. Mair, A. Richards and potentially P. Kirchhoff, a total of twenty-four which included 'Mr and Mrs Davis' (the distinguished Black American, Alison Davis), occasionally the sociologist, Talcott Parsons, and others.[5] Not all the members of the seminar were aiming to work in Africa; his students, Fei and Hsu, followed at the School by Tien Jukung, were important in extending social anthropology to China. But as the result of the benefactions of the Rockefeller Foundation much of the research of the School was directed to that continent, to the study of which the majority of the Fellows contributed important monographs. There can rarely have been a more effective use of funds in the history of research in the social sciences.

The programme was very much in line with the aims of the Rockefeller Memorial and later the Foundation to encourage co-operative groups on a more systematic and empirical basis, at the same time as breaking down old subject divisions.[6] Day, for example, was wary of 'many of the prescriptions of capitalistic individualism'.[7] That programme was to establish centres of excellence, to which they would bring advanced students by offering them fellowships to 'receive training in scientific methods and be allowed the freedom to conduct their own research'.[8] That policy, outlined in Ruml's memorandum submitted to the Memorial in 1922 and in the Frank Report, was aimed at consolidating and professionalising the academic social sciences, which is exactly what happened with British social anthropology, although the contradiction was, as Fisher points out, that the process itself involves erecting new disciplinary barriers.

The letter Malinowski addressed to Oldham about prospective students reminded him that he had already spoken about 'the South African Ukrainian Jew named Fortes. He is perhaps for sheer brilliancy and real capacity and intelligence the best pupil I have ever had.' He had come with glowing recommendations from Flügel, the psycho-analyst at University College, but since he was judged not to be dogmatically committed to that approach, he was acceptable. 'I want you ...', he wrote to Oldham, 'to take him into your little fold.' Meanwhile Malinowski said he was arranging for him to go to the States to work with Radcliffe-Brown for a session, probably at Fortes' insistence, after which he would return to spend the academic year 1932–3 at the London School of Economics. 'Don't be put off', he told Oldham, 'by his manners ... which are South African, nor by his ideas, which are a little Eastern European ghetto.' The significance of these remarks was brought out later when it came to considering Fortes' proposal for fieldwork, in his difficulties in getting into the Gold Coast, as well as in his ambiguous position, situated between Malinowski and Radcliffe-Brown. While Malinowski's comments may appear full of prejudice, given his style of writing they cannot be altogether taken as evidence of anti-Semitism on his part. It would be wrong to read his verbal statements in a way that one would those of a more reserved character. In writing to the Social Science Research Council (US) about Frank Meyer, one of the founders of the October Club in Oxford and a member of his seminar, he remarks that 'His drawbacks are that he is a Jew and has strong leanings towards the left.'[9] He says virtually the same of Fortes and others, including Evans-Pritchard at that period. At the same time he is equally uncomplimentary about French and Germans, insisting on his stance as a Polish nobleman but affecting the extreme attitudes of a true Anglo-Saxon that 'wogs begin at Calais'. I say 'affecting' because it appears in some ways as a mask, for it certainly does not prevent him from devoting his teaching time as well as a great deal of extra-mural support to Jews and Reds, clearly numbering them among his best friends. He also spoke six European languages fluently and always remained a foreigner in England. The written word has always to be understood in relation to the personality and social systems of the actor, but in Malinowski's case this was a relationship of great complexity.

Fortes had attended South African College School, Cape Town, between 1918 and 1922, and moved to the University of Cape Town in 1923, remaining there until 1927. He took the BA with distinction in 1925, obtaining the Noble Scholarship for the best graduate of the year, and passed the MA in 1926, when he received the highest post-graduate scholarship of the year. He came to London in 1927, registered for a PhD and worked under Professor Spearman at University College. His future wife, Sonia, came to London to be married in 1928 and he took his PhD in 1930. He was awarded the Ratan Tata Research Studentship at the London School of Economics in that year and continued to be attached, now to the School rather than University College, as a part-time student for a further PhD.

His preliminary application for a Rockefeller Fellowship in December 1931 gave as his referees the mathematician, Professor Lancelot Hogben, whom he had known personally since 1927, the psychiatrist, Dr Emanuel Miller (since 1928), and the sociologist, Professor Morris Ginsberg, whom he had met intermittently since the same year and who had introduced him to Miller. The application was supported in a lukewarm fashion by the psychologist, Professor Bartlett at Cambridge, whom he had just met, as well as by Radcliffe-Brown and by Seligman, both of whom he had encountered through Evans-Pritchard. But the strongest recommendation came from Evans-Pritchard himself who described him as 'a first-class man' with 'a quite exceptional critical ability', who was especially keen on the study of culture contact. A knowledge of Evans-Pritchard's views on the subject makes it seem that the latter remark was made very much tongue in cheek, aimed to please the providers of funds, although that interest was certainly strong not only for Fortes but others of his South African contemporaries, such as Schapera and Gluckman.

Owing to Fortes' position in relation to Malinowski and Radcliffe-Brown, there was a tug-of-war about where he would study. Radcliffe-Brown wrote from Chicago in support of his application in February 1932, saying that he had already made two attempts to get Fortes to come to Chicago; one failed because the university did not have the money, the other because the normal Rockefeller awards were not available to South Africans. Radcliffe-Brown claimed to have formed a high opinion of Fortes based on interviews and because the psychologist, Reyburn, at the University of Cape Town where Radcliffe-Brown himself had taught, regarded him as his best student, but thought he needed further training before doing fieldwork in Africa, possibly at Johannesburg with Hoernlé (a former student of Radcliffe-Brown).

As it turned out, the plan to go to Chicago did not work out and Fortes had to remain with Malinowski in London, which was where the Fellowships were based. His first research proposal, two quarto pages in length, was sent to Malinowski, who had already talked to Noel Hall of the Rockefeller Foundation about the possibility of getting a Fellowship for him, although the psychologist, Flügel, was his official nominator.[10] The proposal began: 'My object is to study the primitive child, in the setting of his family and community, by observational methods which have hitherto been used only with civilised children.' He goes on to state that he has been trying to do a sociological study in the East End of London for the past six months and would like to do comparative work on primitive children using 'the methods of functional anthropology' to solve psychological problems, that means beginning with 'a sociological analysis of the child's domestic, cultural, and community setting, and then proceeding to study the child's behaviour in this setting'. Obviously Fortes had already been influenced by the ideas of Malinowski whom he had met at Flügel's house earlier in 1931, before he ever formally studied with him.[11]

In his final application for a Fellowship, dated March of the following year, Fortes describes his part-time activities as a PhD student at the London School of Economics, as a lecturer at the London County Council Evening Institute from 1929 and as a psychologist at the East London Child Guidance Clinic, attached from 1928 to the Jew's Hospital, the Head of which was Dr Emanuel Miller. Evidence of the debt which Fortes owed to the association with this psychiatrist is provided by the fact that he was later to give the first Emanuel Miller memorial lecture to the Association for Child Psychology and Psychiatry in 1972 under the title of 'The first-born'.

Already in October 1931 the Executive Committee of the International African Institute meeting in Paris had been told of the candidates for Fellowships and Fortes was number one on the list. They were informed that he 'wishes to study anthropology for a year and then go out to Africa to work on the psychology of native children and to make some attempt at standardizing intelligence tests for natives', the subject on which he had worked for his PhD. He was ready to adopt numerical experimental techniques as well as to analyse 'the exact place of individuality'. At this point in his programme emphasis was placed on experimental psychology in an African setting, but that was to change under the influence of functional anthropology and of the social psychological research he had been carrying out in the East End. For, although Fortes' application for an award was accepted, the Institute memorandum he submitted did not greatly please his future teacher. The Institute discussed the memo in February 1932, and found it 'not very lively', as Oldham reported to Malinowski, asking 'Is he past the clever young man stage and ready to do some work?'[12] Malinowski replied from Toulon, telling the Secretary, Dorothy Brackett, whose influence was very strong, that Fortes was making other plans but was not yet ready to go to Africa and should work with him for another full year.[13] In other words Fortes had to stay under the master's tutelage for longer than he expected.

To Oldham Malinowski wrote in stronger terms. He claimed to have known Fortes for three to four years during which time 'he has improved greatly', but he is still 'impossible'. 'I know that politically he is wrong-headed, I know that he has started as an absolutely impossibly arrogant South African Jew; I know he has improved and is damnably clever. But I don't know whether he can work and produce ...'[14] About Fortes' memorandum he was even more scathing; 'I regard it as preposterous – any clever journalist could write 200 such memoranda over the weekend. In his memorandum, that is, there is no single concrete and founded statement, only promises and good intentions, and even these pretty badly expressed.' The next sentence indicates a more immediate source of his concern. 'He has been rather rude and impertinent but it is better he works here with me than go to R.B.' Clearly this was part of the problem for both men. Fortes wanted to work with Radcliffe-Brown for at least part of the time, influenced no doubt by Evans-Pritchard. In the end he had to stay in London. Malinowski arranged for him, Nadel and Wilson to get 'special coaching' from Audrey Richards and he had apparently extracted a promise from Fortes to work with him for a year, that is, 1932–3.[15] In March 1932 Fortes wrote saying that he had already spent a year on 'sociological studies', indicating his impatience to get on with research or else to get away from Malinowski, possibly both. But Malinowski held the purse-strings and said he could not recommend him for a

Fellowship unless he kept his promise.[16] Malinowski persuaded
Oldham to press the Foundation to allow Fortes to study in Britain,
since he could then learn the languages (he was later in touch with
Westermann at Berlin about learning Twi) and could get in contact
with Edwin Smith, Rattray and others, who had worked in the Gold
Coast.[17] Those purse-strings opened wider when Kirchhoff, another
Fellow, was prevented from going to Africa. For it was on the same day
that Oldham wrote to Malinowski saying: 'Now that we have lost
Kirchhoff I should be glad to go ahead with Fortes.'[18] As will become
clear, the reasons for the sudden vacancy were central to the history of
Fortes' research. The recommendation for a fellowship for Fortes was
put before the Executive Council in July 1932. For this meeting another
memorandum was submitted, dated 26 March 1932, which begins
'Somewhere in his well-known article on Anthropology in the
Encyclopaedia Britannica, Professor Malinowski remarks ...' The
obeisance, as Evans-Pritchard saw it, paid off, though Fortes was
genuinely attracted to Malinowski's work. Meanwhile it was announced
at the meeting that Fortes, described as 'a brilliant psychologist' with
'excellent recommendations', had just been given a ten-month Fellowship by the Rockefeller Foundation to study in London (an exception,
as South Africans were not included in their normal schemes) on
condition that the International African Institute subsequently awarded
him a fellowship for field research, which in turn they did.

Other Fellows were elected at the same time. In each case the
condition of receiving their grant was that they received a training in
anthropology under Malinowski since his links with the International
African Institute were so close. The three Fellows, Fortes, Nadel and
Hofstra, the first two of whom became known as the Mandarins, were
actually to be given instruction in anthropology under both Malinowski
and Seligman, though the latter seems to have been a formal addition.
All three already had PhDs, Fortes in psychology, Nadel in the same
(Vienna 1925, specialising in music) and Hofstra in anthropology. All
three intended to work in West Africa, Fortes with his wife Sonia, who
had been a fellow-student in Cape Town, where she had come from
the Soviet Union. Eventually Fortes, Nadel and their wives set sail to
West Africa on the same ship in December 1933, while Hofstra went to
Sierra Leone in the following month.

Malinowski regarded supervision as an exclusive relationship; it was
a task he could not share with anyone else. In June 1932 he sent a
memorandum to the Rockefeller Foundation entitled 'On the exclusive

supervision of fieldwork by one teacher'. The immediate cause was the fact that Lucy Mair, who was in Africa on a ten-month field trip, had been receiving advice from her mother (the Secretary of the School), from Beveridge (the Director) and from Coatman (who later wrote supporting Fortes' entry to the Gold Coast). In the field Malinowski objected to her moving about from one group to another, a practice of which he strongly disapproved in Seligman's students.[19] He objected even more strongly to interference from others. He wrote to Mrs Mair protesting that she had sent a cable to her daughter using his name and calling her back six weeks before the anticipated end of her research; 'fieldwork', he insisted, 'is not a sinecure nor a form of exotic entertainment'.[20]

What did his pre-fieldwork training consist of? Writing to Hofstra, who was about to join him, Malinowski said, 'I would like you to become acquainted with the work of the French sociological school of Durkheim.'[21] That advice would have sounded more characteristic had it come from Radcliffe-Brown since the work of the French school appears to have made less impact on Malinowski's writings. Nevertheless Fortes also characterised himself as pursuing 'sociological studies' when working with him, and this was certainly one way in which his teacher characterised his own work. However, for Malinowski training consisted principally of participation in his seminars which were usually based on an analysis of fieldwork, either his own or that of other participants.

So their formal activity consisted mainly of going to his lively seminars which were attended by colleagues, students and a number of visitors. In these they had to present their plans and later their findings before a critical audience of peers. It was a kind of collective apprenticeship, the form of which was later copied at Oxford under Evans-Pritchard, then at Manchester and Cambridge under Gluckman and Fortes respectively. The discussion often centred upon the collection of data in the context of social action and its analysis in the framework of the social system as a whole. Usually it did not finish in the classroom but continued afterwards in a café or pub. In addition students were encouraged to read sociological theory, the ethnographic literature on the area to be studied and to acquire whatever necessary language skills were available.

They were also taught to present their data not only verbally but in the form of analytic tables, such as are scattered through the numerous studies of his students. This technique can lead to unnecessary formalisations, even the tabulation of absurdities, but tables were also useful ways of summarising field data, of pointing to gaps in the record and of leading generatively to new perspectives.

In addition they were taught 'field methods', though it has to be said that most of these bordered on the simple-minded. Audrey Richards has described how Malinowski recommended using different coloured pencils for notes on different topics. While such techniques are of limited use, they do help to keep track of the multifarious material that the observers were asked to record in their field notebooks. The holistic approach that Malinowski advocated meant taking notes on the whole range of human interaction; that was implied in methodological functionalism. It entailed examining the interrelations between the different aspects of social life, between politics and religion, between family and the economy. All this had to be carried out by one research worker and possibly an assistant, so that much emphasis was placed on systematic methods; that tendency was especially noticeable among those who later worked with Gluckman at the Rhodes–Livingstone Institute. The result was a series of excellent ethnographic accounts of African societies, to which most of his students made substantial contributions.

Malinowski was often critical about his new students, though he appreciated their efforts. Of Fortes and his wife he wrote to Oldham that 'they are keeping up to expectations which, as you know, were fairly high'. Nadel he regarded as very capable and brilliant, 'but not without some rather difficult continental mannerisms i.e. argumentative, running into unproductive abstract discussions'.[22]

When Fortes, Nadel and Hofstra came under Malinowski's direction for the academic year 1932–3, they had been asked to work together on the study of culture contact and to elaborate the necessary techniques. The choice of topic was of course dictated by the Rockefeller Foundation. While that topic had little influence on their main research, it did lead to a number of publications on the subject. However, at the end of the period of training the Directors asked them to submit a joint memorandum on Schemes of Research, plus individual statements on the proposal for 'practical anthropology', all of which were put before the Bureau of the International African Institute at a meeting held after the three Fellows had already left for West Africa.[23]

The documents, which are given in Appendix 1, make interesting reading because they testify to the strong influence that Malinowski (and others at his seminars) had on these proposals, as well as to the strength of 'functionalist paradigms' at a purely theoretical level. However much of what they absorbed was not so much functionalism as usually defined but rather a formalising, systematising approach to social facts, together with the need for a continuing attempt to relate institutions to one another, at the level of individual action, of the group and of the domain or sub-system.

It is also interesting to look at the changing nature of the individual research proposals under the influence of Malinowski's teaching and, later on, the changing nature of the research itself as field circumstances impinge upon plans, interests and ideas. Fortes' first proposal, as presented to the meeting of the Executive Council of the Institute, was basically psychological, though certainly not psychoanalytical, partly aimed at the development of cross-cultural intelligence tests, a subject on which he had already been influenced by Malinowski. Nadel's first proposal, presented to the London meeting of the Executive Council in July 1932, centred upon music – he had already worked on archives of recordings in Vienna, where he was born, as well as in Berlin, where he was then living, apparently unable to continue his work in anti-Semitic Austria. His research was to be in 'African ethnography and fieldwork, in order to increase ethnographically and practically the knowledge of music'.

In keeping with the emphasis on group work, the three Fellows produced a joint memorandum at the end of their training period, followed by three separate statements; Fortes' was entitled 'Sketch of a plan for the study of the African Family', Nadel's was a 'Scheme for the investigation of religious institutions', and Hofstra worked out a 'Scheme for a study of secret societies'. The joint memorandum given in Appendix 1 was subdivided into three sections, (1) Classification of social facts, (2) Function and relation of institutions, (3) Problems of psychological factors. It ends by noting that 'the best practical means of presenting the concrete application of the points of view elaborated above are diagrammatic schemes as suggested by Professor Malinowski in his Seminar'. In Fortes' own memorandum he talks of 'basic needs', a Malinowskian formulation of one aspect of his approach, and goes on to point to the role of the ancestor cult in social cohesion; Edith Clarke, another student of Malinowski, wrote in similar terms of Asante ancestor worship contributing to social solidarity, a theme taken up by Fortes in his first paper on fishing magic. Fortes then speaks of 'sentiments of respect for authority in the family', of the importance of the 'ritual of family life' (e.g. funerals), as well as of the necessity of looking at the family along the 'time co-ordinate', biographically. In more general terms he perceived the links between the personality system and the social system (to employ Parsons' terms) as in need of exploration. In other words, a number of ideas which he developed later on were already being sketched out, the role of familial cults, of the developmental cycle, of domestic authority, of the interlocking nature of sociological and psychological enquiry.

The memorandum contained an acknowledgement of the help of Malinowski but that proved not to be sufficient for their teacher. He immediately expressed an objection to Oldham, though he waited before bringing it up with the students themselves. The joint document, which he had been sent as a member of Council, 'is in a way a fake, or more exactly a partial plagiarism. It is really more a summary of my teaching which the three fellows received over the last eighteen months.'[25] That complaint is itself an indication of how much his students had 'learnt' from him.

When the three Research Fellows had established themselves in the field, they sent back regular reports. Malinowski wanted them monthly but Fortes' first statement was dated three months after he had got to the field,[26] and the second was four months later. Nadel did not report until 5 May and he was regarded as the best fieldworker.[27] Hofstra on the other hand suffered from ill health and his performance left something to be desired.

All three returned for a period in 1935. During this time they again attended Malinowski's seminar. The session began by laying out the elements of social organisation.[28] 'Tradition, culture, society, mean the same thing', it was proclaimed, so stick to 'culture'. Culture consisted of the following elements arranged in a specific way:
Education
Government – war – political organisation
Language
Economics – crafts
Material culture
Religion – magic
Social organisation
Law – morality – custom
Later on in the session Fortes made a contribution on 'The culture scheme and the fieldworker', taking funerals as his case material and being more concerned to differentiate tradition, culture and society

rather than to lump them together.[29] At this time Malinowski was trying to elaborate in a more explicit fashion his 'functional theory' (of culture) which he began to oppose directly to the functionalism of Durkheim.[30] His approach (or 'theory') was characterised by three factors:

(a) the elaboration of 'a sort of inventory of the elements of culture',
(b) a belief in the 'wholeness of culture', none of the elements receiving any special emphasis,
(c) and the idea of 'fieldwork as experimental testing of a theoretical approach'.

Only perhaps in the context of the highly fragmented amateur ethnographies of earlier times would remarks of this level of generality have much to offer the budding anthropologist and it is difficult now to see what could have been borrowed by sophisticated social scientists. Nevertheless Malinowski felt that in writing up their initial proposals for the field, Fortes, Nadel and Hofstra had plagiarised him, as he had pointed out to Oldham in 1934. Two years later he returned to the matter and wrote to Fortes asking that the Fellows once again insert the original acknowledgement to his seminar which had been included in the joint document circulated to the International African Institute, because he now wanted to publish some of the ideas. He even enclosed a draft of what he wanted.[31] This may well be the occasion referred to by Meyer Fortes when he told me that Malinowski had once asked him to acknowledge in writing that all his ideas were borrowed from him.[32] At another time Fortes referred to the contributions made by students to Malinowski's writing up, as well as to his research generally. There does seem to have been a considerable *quid pro quo*. While no-one would attribute most of Fortes' ideas to his teacher, the research documents that were prepared by the three as a result of their year's work differ considerably from the original proposals they had submitted and bear very strong marks of Malinowski's teaching, partly in their functional vocabulary and the desire to see things working in an interlocking way (as they appear in fieldwork), but more especially in the sociological questions they were asking and in the degree of formalisation of the results, rather than on the more superficial level of 'elements', of socio-cultural phenomena. They tried to look, as Fortes would later say, at systematic relationships. In his own account of his training, which he called 'An anthropologist's apprenticeship', he described his encounter with Malinowski whose 'catalytic virtuosity kept the seminar at a high pitch'.[33] While he later said that they were not impressed with his claims for functionalism, 'all agreed that it represented a revolution in fieldwork method'. But an important element of Malinowski's theoretical influence lay at a different level, in encouraging the examination of more concrete problems. For example, since the Trobriands were matrilineal he became interested in the general attributes of such systems, both at the societal and interpersonal levels. It is not accidental that two of those who worked with him – Richards among the Bemba, Fortes among the Ashanti – made very substantial contributions to the study of such societies not only of the organisation of that type of kin group and to the concomitant problems of residence, ownership and marriage, but to the interpersonal tensions that marked particular kinds of matrilineal system.

Malinowski's ability to gather round him a group of students lay partly in his profound commitment to the subject and to the intensity of his belief in the value of field research. Intellectually he clearly played a great part in redirecting the research of Fortes, Nadel and many others. But it was also the case that he held the purse-strings in his own hands through his friendship with Oldham at the Institute and through his contacts with the Rockefeller Foundation; in both quarters his reputation was high, not least because he displayed an interest in 'practical anthropology' as distinct from the purely academic variety.

It was also practical in the further sense that his correspondence shows him to have been at the centre of numerous manœuvres to place people in jobs. In June 1933 he wrote to the Rockefeller Foundation of his deep conviction that the future of linguistics lay 'in the study of meaning connected with the study of phonetics' and asked for a lectureship for J. R. Firth, described as 'the coming man'. He placed much emphasis on linguistics, partly because fieldwork required the learning of a language but also because he was interested in theoretical aspects of language and wrote an important appendix to *The Meaning of Meaning* (1923) by those key figures in interwar intellectual life in Britain, C. K. Ogden and I. A. Richards; the interest in meaning was intrinsic to his field studies. At the same time as he wrote on behalf of Firth he requested a post for Audrey Richards.[34] In the following year, 1934, he wrote to the Rockefeller asking for money to go to see his students in Africa as well as for Reo Fortune, whom he had backed for the proposed Chair of Sociology at Cambridge;[35] Fortune was attending his seminars at the time and had asked Malinowski to write an introduction to his valuable ethnographic study, *The Sorcerers of Dobu* (1932).

But Malinowski's major interest was in practical anthropology of another kind, which, while offering help to colonial governments as well as to the governed, inevitably led to a series of conflicts. The research programme meant recruiting intellectuals from various countries whose views on society were in many cases strongly influenced by the political climate of Europe in the early thirties, by the economic depression, by the rise of Fascism and by the growth of communism. These were the people he required to carry out the programme of practical anthropology elaborated in conjunction with the Rockefeller Foundation. Much has been made in recent years of the role of British anthropologists working under colonial regimes, supported by a conservative social theory known as structural-functionalism. Some of this criticism has emanated from members or supporters of the two major world powers, European in origin, that have managed to subdue and incorporate, temporarily at least, the native populations of the areas in Russia and North America into which they expanded. But the attempt to show structural-functionalism as the necessary ideology of the colonial regimes and anthropologists as their instruments comes up against a number of difficulties when we look at the actual history of the participants, for in many cases their attitudes and roles were very different from what these holistic assumptions would predict. That is because such pronouncements ignore the internal contradictions of colonial rule as well as the relative autonomy (however limited) of fields of knowledge. Both before and after the Second World War a number of anthropologists were excluded from or had great problems in getting access to the colonies, while most others were concerned not so much to support colonial rule as to modify or even abolish it. One clear example is the case of Meyer Fortes who faced considerable difficulties in getting into what was then the Protectorate of the Northern Territories of the Gold Coast, now part of the independent nation of Ghana.

The problem of entry into colonial territories had already arisen with missionaries and even with traders but never with academics. In anglophone West Africa professional anthropology began with the appointment of existing members of the colonial service as government anthropologists. There were few of these: R. S. Rattray who worked among the Asante of Ghana, Meek among the Ibo of Nigeria – figures who were the rough equivalents of Tauxier in the Côte d'Ivoire and H. Labouret in what is now Burkina Faso. In both France and Britain, colonial officers received some training in anthropology, Cambridge providing teaching from 1906 and starting a Diploma in 1908 with such professional courses very much in mind. Mauss gave similar instruction in Paris. So that apart from those of the specialists like Rattray, a number of contributions were made by other district officers like Cardinall in his works on the Gold Coast, especially when, as the result of the extension of the system of indirect rule, they were expected to write essays on aspects of the social organisation of local peoples. These appeared in the early 1930s and often constitute useful pieces of ethnographic research, many of which were deposited with the Royal Anthropological Institute in London. But it has to be said that there was little in the anglophone areas comparable to the kind of historical, linguistic and ethnographic survey contained in say Delafosse's 'Haute-Sénégal-Niger' (1912) or Clozel's volume on the customary law of the Côte d'Ivoire (1902). One might suggest that this was a matter of scale, with France dominating West Africa. But early German research in Togo and the Cameroons displays a similarly high quality; from the end of the nineteenth century, the journals of the *Deutscheschutzgebiet* are full of interesting papers by Herr Doktor this and that. These people often carried out their research with a notebook in one hand and a machine-gun in the other, for their colonial procedures were usually more aggressive than those of the dominant colonial powers – necessarily so, from one point of view, for they felt that they had to carve out for themselves by force a *Lebensraum* since their rivals had long established bases in the region from which they could operate in a more leisurely fashion. What was the reason for this relative backwardness of scholarly research in British West Africa? The conventional answer is that the area meant less to the metropolitan country than in the case of France or Germany. The best British administrators, those with the best degrees from Oxbridge, as well as the weight of overseas scholarly interest, were directed to the Jewel in the Crown, India, rather than to the less glamorous Dark Continent. The first two William Wyse Professors at Cambridge had been members of the Indian Civil Service associated with the census; census taking and ethnography went hand in hand as in Cardinall's work in the 1931 Gold Coast Census. It is also the case, in my view, that the Durkheim school in France provided a better basis for such activities than did the contributions of Tylor and Frazer, Perry and Elliot Smith, which were largely concerned with speculations concerning early developments in the history of mankind – not a useless activity by any means but of less relevance in increasing the knowledge of the contemporary 'natives'.

There were of course others such as W. H. R. Rivers who contributed both theoretically, in *Kinship and Social Organisation*, published in 1914, and ethnographically in his work on the Todas of South India, not to speak of the later work of Malinowski, who published *The Argonauts of the Western Pacific* in 1922 and Radcliffe-Brown whose study, *The Andaman Islanders*, appeared in the same year, as well as the work of Charles and Brenda Seligman. But while Paris saw the early embodiment of Durkheimian sociology into the training of future commandants, London had little influence on Oxbridge where the majority of colonial officers were educated. It was only with the dominance of Malinowski that the situation changed, when he started to train career anthropologists rather than colonial officers. The outlook for British professional anthropology in West Africa was profoundly altered in December 1932 when Fortes and Nadel set sail in the same boat for the Guinea Coast.

The local government was not altogether prepared. Rattray has been described as the Gold Coast's 'first government anthropologist', of whom it has been said that his appointment established an official anthropological orientation that persisted long after his retirement in 1931.[36] Rattray's official position had come about because of his long-standing interest in African languages and cultures, which made it possible for him to move within the administration and to become an 'anthropologist' later in life. But far from establishing an official orientation, this administration, like others in Africa, was heavily split in its attitude to the subject. Field officers did not encourage outside research in the social sciences, at least until the period after the Second World War when both the climate of opinion and the views of the junior personnel had greatly changed. Nor were colonial governments very interested in outside research, preferring to get it done by their own staff. That was not necessarily the view of the Colonial Office, which was directly responsible to Parliament and more sensitive to public opinion. But it made for difficulties for academic research, which was exactly why the Rockefeller Foundation thought that the International African Institute could be a valuable intermediary. That turned out to be so, even if they were not always successful.

CHAPTER 3

Making it to the field as a Jew and a Red

The position of anthropologists in relation to foundations, to other sources of funding and to the colonial authorities is brought out very forcefully in the story of Fortes' efforts to get to the field and carry out his research. Even with the collaboration of the International African Institute with the Rockefeller philanthropies on the one hand and the Colonial Office on the other, there were many difficulties in undertaking fieldwork, about whose merits opinions differed.

The Rockefeller plan called for the study of culture contact. The scheme was intended to be relevant to current issues, not to concern itself with antiquarian matters. Malinowski later wrote that they 'had been training young men and women in practical anthropology'.[1] An internal memo of March 1938 sums up the intention of the scheme as it had been conceived seven years previously.

After careful consideration the Council of the Institute decided to direct the research to be undertaken towards a better understanding of those aspects of native society making for social cohesion, the economics of communal life, the ways in which African society is being disrupted by the invasion of western ideas and economic forces, and the resulting changes in African institutions and behaviour. Thus the research would be concentrated on problems of most direct concern to colonial governments, educators and others engaged in practical tasks in Africa.

So conditions were laid down that had some influence on subsequent research, but nevertheless the results were not altogether as planned. The Rockefeller Foundation was interested in the effects of culture contact, specifically on native peoples. It was also interested in group projects. It was specifically the wishes (and the funds) of the Rockefeller Foundation that accounted for the attempt to get all the Fellows of the International African Institute to consider this topic, even though that was rarely their main interest. The result was a special number of the journal, *Africa*, devoted to the subject, the focus of a debate between

Malinowski, Fortes and later Gluckman. The latter objected to Malinowski's vision of cultures coming into contact like thunderclouds, preferring to look at the situation in terms of social relationships that partially cross-cut, say, the black and white division in South Africa, as exemplified in Gluckman's analysis of a social situation in Zululand (1958). But the differences lay not simply at the level of theory but also of what one might call morality. Here the main protagonist, Evans-Pritchard, was a romantic as well as a scholar and held his main object to be to get to know and analyse the simpler societies for their own sake. Getting involved in culture contact meant not only neglecting the scholarly task but also having to deal with colonial governments; with them, he used to say, you should only sup with a long spoon, as with the devil. In practice Evans-Pritchard had himself worked closely with the Sudanese government, from whom he received funds as well as favours, though he saw himself as independent. He certainly held ambivalent attitudes, on this as on many other issues.[2] But in my experience his advice to students was unambiguous. Keep right away from the administration.

It hardly needs pointing out that in Africa during the colonial period this advice was as impractical as it is now; the fieldworker is forced to put himself in the hands of some network or other, at least for part of the time. But his insistence on independence did mean that students were encouraged to choose topics in which they themselves rather than the administration were interested. It also meant, less happily, that they often avoided including the District Commissioner in their analysis, say, of the Samo or the Mossi, the Tallensi or the Asante. They kept away too for many years from a direct confrontation with the problems of dramatic social change. That avoidance persisted longer in Britain than in France, where many scholars worked with ORSTOM, a government agency; others like Tardits studied the urban situation in Porto Novo. Such enquiries received little or no encouragement after the war either from Evans-Pritchard at Oxford or from Fortes at Cambridge.

It was much the same with the Institute's Fellows. While their initial proposals referred to social change, few (except perhaps A. I. Richards) paid much attention to the topic, although in South Africa anthropologists like Schapera and Monica Wilson were inevitably forced to discuss the question. The avoidance in Britain was due not only to Evans-Pritchard's objections, nor to the sometimes rather sloppy theoretical approach of Malinowski, but to the fact the independent conditions under which the fellows worked permitted them to follow their own ethnographic interests. In almost every case this freedom led to a concentration on gaining a deeper knowledge of native society rather than to following the lines laid down for the study of 'culture contact'.

The extensive programme of field research demanded the co-operation of the colonial authorities in Africa, the prospect of which had been one of the reasons for the establishment of the Rockefeller project in London. It also demanded the recruitment of a group of first-class students drawn from different nationalities (including South Africans, who were excluded from the ordinary Rockefeller Fellowships). Grounds for conflict were built into the scheme, both in the form of potential opposition between colonial government and the intellectuals of the period, and because the latter were being financed to carry out practical anthropology when their interests as intellectuals lay elsewhere, in more 'academic' or 'theoretical' directions.

The first problem of a group of intellectuals of the 1930s carrying out fieldwork in African colonies was brought to a climax in the case of Paul Kirchhoff. He had come to London for some weeks of study preparatory to going to the field but was eventually told by the Colonial Office that he could not have permission to work in Nyasaland. As a consequence his Institute award was terminated. It was the problem of Kirchhoff that made difficulties for Fortes' entry into Ghana.

Kirchhoff had spent a short while working with Malinowski in 1926, had subsequently been employed by the Rockefeller Foundation in South America for two years and was recommended to the International African Institute by one of its Directors, Diedrich Westermann. He had left Berlin at the beginning of the Hitler regime under which he had been involved in left-wing political activity, but he was strongly supported by members of the Foundation and encouraged to become an Africanist. On coming to London in 1931, he made an excellent impression on his colleagues, as Audrey Richards reported to Malinowski when he was living at Toulon.[3] At first he wanted to go to Basutoland (now Lesotho). Oldham had practical reasons against this choice and suggested he should go to Northern Rhodesia (now Zambia) because of the mining interests. But Malinowski did not approve because Richards was already working there. So Kirchhoff applied to go to Nyasaland (now Malawi) and, since he was judged to be experienced, arrangements went ahead for him to leave right away without the period of training which the others had to undergo.

A few days before he set sail for Africa 'some intelligence service or other' sent a report to the Colonial Office (who had been very helpful up to that point) and he was refused permission to go into any British territory. 'The indictment against him was that he had something to do with communistic views or perhaps propaganda.'[4] Oldham duly reported to Malinowski telling him that his colleague at the Institute, Major H. Vischer, had seen the information. According to Oldham, the Colonial Office had acted properly, for Kirchhoff had kept something back. Moreover, his wife was also involved in what was 'more than a philosophical commitment to Communism, or mere political associations'.[5] Despite the fact that Kirchhoff obtained a certificate of good behaviour from the German police, the Colonial Office refused to consider the matter: 'We know from himself that both here and in Germany he has been mixed up with communism.' However the government claimed to know more.[6] The Institute was therefore not in a position to do what it wanted, as the Secretary, Dorothy Brackett, pointed out, 'without the goodwill of Government'.[7] So it had to cancel his contract and look for money to enable him to return to Berlin, although it would clearly have been unwise for him to do so.[8]

The case of Kirchhoff was worrying to Malinowski not because he disapproved of the Colonial Office vetoing the entry of an active communist, but because the reasons were not made public. He compared the situation with his own in the Trobriands where rumours about him flew around during the First World War. In addition to 'victimisation' he was worried about the repercussions of this action on his research programme, since he was well aware of the leftist inclinations of others of his students.

Take the case of Fortes for instance, I know the boy is or imagines himself to be a Communist and pro-Bolshevik. I have been advising him for some time to look up to the Institute as his future alma mater. But now I have to warn you [he wrote to Oldham] and shall also have to warn him some sort of definite understanding will have to be arrived at with the Colonial Office as to the way in which they will deal with us, and as to the definite conditions which we shall have to impose on our candidates before we accept them.[9]

He demanded clarity, but in fact he went much further.

Despite his disapproval of Kirchhoff's beliefs Malinowski did his best to help him, prompted by Audrey Richards whom Oldham had placed in charge of the newcomer. Richards organised anthropologists in his support and actively looked for another post he could fill. She wrote to T. T. Barnard at the University of Cape Town to see if it would be possible for him to work there. Barnard replied that the university would accept him if she could get the Institute to re-vote the funds they had withdrawn. In this way they could try to get the Colonial Office off the hook. In an attached note, Barnard comments that Richards seemed 'unduly impressed with the powers of the Colonial Office. But they will of course have to be squared.' As things turned out, Richards' fears about its influence were fully justified.[10]

At the same time Malinowski was writing to the linguistic anthropologist, Edward Sapir, at Yale as well as to Raymond Firth in Australia about the possibility of an Oceania Fellowship at Sydney. Firth had inherited Radcliffe-Brown's position as Secretary of the Social Science Committee of the Australian National Research Council. In fact Malinowski wrote two letters on the subject of Kirchhoff on the same day, one official, one personal.[11] In this he claimed, 'The whole [communist] theory is a canard', a view that was apparently based on Seligman's assertion to him a few days before that Kirchhoff 'is not a member of the Communist party, or was not when I last saw him'.[12]

At first there seemed some hope for Kirchhoff in Australia and in September Malinowski reported to the Rockefeller Foundation from Toulon that he would receive a generous allowance for fieldwork.[13] But on his return to London shortly afterwards, he was met by Audrey Richards 'who has been in charge of Kirchhoff's affairs'. She told him a cable had been received from the Chairman of the Australian Research Council withdrawing the award, since the Australian Government had informed the Council that they had been warned about Kirchhoff by the British authorities.[14] Malinowski's reaction was strong. 'I shall set everybody I can in motion, and either discover that Kirchhoff is really a criminal communist, or find something for him.' Indeed he had already spoken to someone 'in touch with the C.I.D.' When the papers came from Australia, he sent them to his friend Oldham for advice, 'feeling rather uncomfortable about the surreptitiousness of the whole affair'.[15]

Malinowski had supported Kirchhoff from the beginning. He thought it 'unlikely that he should be a Bolshevik agent of a dangerous type; more likely he might have been a little silly once or twice, or perhaps convivial'.[16] He even wrote to Kirchhoff saying, 'I cannot believe that a man of your common sense could be a Bolshevik agent.'[17] He later concluded that it was all 'an official error ... probably backed up by one of the political heads of the Colonial Office, who is an extreme diehard conservative as well as notoriously a fool (I mean, of course, Sir Philip Cunliffe-Lister)' whom he already suspected of further victimisation, preventing Kirchhoff from going to Australia.[18] The tentacles of the Colonial Office spread very wide and Kirchhoff eventually had to move right outside their range.

Malinowski had become heavily involved in the affair. Kirchhoff was staying in his London home while he was away, being supported by a group of anthropologists, although he also received a grant of $600 from the Rockefeller Foundation.[19] He was awarded a grant-in-aid to enable him to join the seminar group the following year.[20] However, by the beginning of 1933 Malinowski notes that Kirchhoff has largely dropped out of the group of research students as 'his linguistic interests seem to make functional anthropology of little interest to him'.[21] In May 1933 he reports Kirchhoff going to Ireland to see about fieldwork in connection with the Harvard Sociological Study of County Clare under Lloyd Warner (who had worked with Radcliffe-Brown in Australia), since he could no longer return to Germany.[22] The following year, 1934, Evans-Pritchard met him in Paris where he had a job at the Trocadero Museum, and concluded ' it was not so bad from that point of view'.[23]

Kirchhoff was certainly involved in left-wing politics as his history both before and after this incident attests. But the immediate point is that his case showed the political colours and the solidarity of the anthropologists at the London School of Economics, as well as the difficulties some of them had with the Colonial Office, and especially with the individual colonial governments, in getting to the field. That was especially true in the case of Meyer Fortes.

To some extent Fortes benefited from Kirchhoff's disappearance from the scene, since it created a vacancy in the Fellowship programme. At the same time the precedent caused him serious difficulties. He had sent his proposal to Malinowski in July 1931 and submitted an application to the Institute at the end of December. On January 1932, Oldham wrote to Malinowski asking him for a letter about Fortes including comments on the memorandum he had submitted, saying at the same time that a decision on the grant had been postponed. It was just then that the Kirchhoff affair blew up.

Malinowski replied on 5 February, mentioning Fortes' pro-Bolshevik leanings, and on the 16th Oldham again wrote for a recommendation, asking that he make no mention of that subject since the matter was best raised in conversation (for he had invited Fortes to dinner) and in any case the Colonial Office had 'not heard anything to his disadvantage'.[24] Oldham was satisfied with the results of his enquiries and observations and his conclusions appear to have been accepted by Malinowski who on 3 March wrote about Fortes saying, 'I am far less tolerant of any communistic ideas and propaganda than you are, indeed I feel very strongly about it.' Had he had any strong objections he would have raised them at this stage.[25] So Fortes' name was put forward to the Council in July and he received an award for the preliminary year, though on other grounds there was still a measure of uncertainty about his subsequent research, since as late as September Malinowski writes that 'We have been dangling that bait before Fortes for twelve months.'[26]

Meanwhile, as early as March of that year Fortes had been getting impatient, wanting to get off to the field. Writing from Toulon, Malinowski reminds him that they had agreed to work together for the year 1932–3 and he could not recommend him for one of the Fellowships of the International African Institute to carry out fieldwork unless he fulfilled his side of the bargain. Fortes replied immediately, referring to 'another misunderstanding between us' but after pointing out that he had already spent a year 'in sociological studies', he agreed to wait until December 1933. There was already tension between the benefactor (or patron) and the recipient (or client).

At an early stage Oldham wrote to the Governor of the Gold Coast, Sir Ransford Slater, outlining the proposal for Fortes to work there and in February 1932 he received a reply that was 'generally favourable to the project'.[27] When he returned to England in June 1932 Oldham arranged for Fortes to meet both Slater who had been the Governor since 1927, as well as his successor, Shenton Thomas. Slater was impressed by Fortes' 'youth, keenness, common sense and readiness to accept suggestions' as well as by his research project. Another virtue in his eyes was that, 'though South African born, he evidently does not hold the common South African attitude towards the native, which makes him suitable for the Gold Coast'. In writing about this interview, Slater recommended that a start be made on the formal approach to the Colonial Office so that they could make any enquiries they might deem desirable. As a result Oldham wrote at once to the Secretary of

State for the Colonies, W. C. Bottomley. The reason for this caution was that the very first Fellow to be appointed by the Institute had been Kirchhoff, who was to have worked in the British Protectorate of Nyasaland of which Shenton Thomas had unfortunately been Governor at the time. Because of the protests that followed his exclusion from Africa, especially on the part of the London School of Economics, the Colonial Office was in some trouble and the Institute had therefore become 'more than ordinarily careful in regard to the selection of our candidates'.[28]

When Oldham asked Bottomley to ensure he was safe in proceeding with Fortes, investigations were made 'in the authoritative quarters'. Since no black marks had been recorded he was told that 'Fortes was all right'[29] and it was arranged that the applicant should have tea with the new Governor at his club. However, at roughly the same time, Vischer, the Secretary-General of the Institute, informed the Colonial Office that at one of its recent meetings they had been told that Fortes 'made a special point of telling his fellow students at the London School of Economics that he was a communist', gilding the lily by pointing out that he was married to 'a Russian lady'. Shenton Thomas was given this information just after his interview with Fortes and so made no further report, thinking the whole matter was closed. The source of Vischer's information on Fortes is unclear, but it may well have arisen out of remarks Malinowski made to Oldham in the light of the Kirchhoff affair. These Vischer would have duly reported, being 'in the pay of the Colonial Office'; he had earlier worked in West Africa as a Colonial Officer and continued to be their man. However this may be, the project now bristled with difficulties. Knowing nothing of these complications, Oldham thought the coast was clear and in March 1933 formally applied to the Colonial Office on behalf of Fortes for permission to undertake 'sociological research'. At the same time he wrote to Shenton Thomas as Governor of the Gold Coast asking that the application be favourably received, for although Fortes might be 'somewhat lacking in personal charm', he was a man of quite unusual ability, of sound judgement, and one whose work would be of interest to the government as well as being an original contribution to sociology. He reminded Thomas that he had met Fortes in London earlier in the year. The response was explosive. Shenton Thomas expressed his objections in a handwritten comment to his assistant on Oldham's letter about Fortes' entry which reads: 'You had better keep this in the D.C.'s cupboard. Fortes struck me as a particularly nasty type of Jew!'[30] He replied in more measured terms to Oldham[31] but made it clear that the 'handicap', to which Oldham referred, would prevent him getting on with Europeans and natives alike. At the same time the Governor wrote to Fiddian at the Colonial Office reminding him that he had spoken about Fortes' communistic views. But his objections went further than the overtly political. 'I don't want him whether communist or not.'[32] This letter crossed with one from Creasey at the Colonial Office forwarding the formal application from the Institute and reminding the Governor that Creasey had told him the previous summer of the report of Fortes' communistic tendencies and of his reply that 'no one who was even suspected of communist views should be allowed to visit the Gold Coast'.[33] However, as further enquiries had provided no support for the rumour, the Secretary of State had agreed to his going on condition that 'fresh enquiries would be made' towards the time of his departure ('October or November next') and that 'even if the result of these further enquiries was satisfactory, Dr Fortes could only go on the distinct understanding that if he were suspected of subversive activities, he would be promptly expelled from the Colony'. The future enquiries were to include Mrs Fortes who is, 'we understand, a Russian lady'. The source of the allegations pointed directly to Vischer.

After going to see the Colonial Office, Oldham replied at length to the Governor's letter, explaining how, in January of the previous year, he had requested Bottomley at the Colonial Office to make enquiries about Fortes and had been told that these were 'entirely satisfactory'.[34] Only some months later did Bottomley indicate that he had 'some less favourable information' (presumably that supplied by Vischer) but agreed that in view of the assurances he had received, 'if nothing further occurred no difficulties would be raised'. It was as a result of these queries that Oldham took his own steps to satisfy himself. He had Fortes and his wife to stay three times, as well as meeting him at Lord Lugard's. 'I have had many hours of intimate conversation with him and I am certain that communism has no attractions for him. He has, in fact, an intellectual contempt for its principles. His interest is wholly scientific and I can imagine nothing more remote from his purpose than to instil political ideas in the mind of the natives ... I have been extremely impressed by the accounts of what he has been doing in the East End and by his understanding and appreciation of work of the church and of social agencies.'[35] If Fortes had any association with communism, it was as a devil's advocate; meanwhile Fortes was 'in all respects admirable and harmless'.[36] Oldham was quite convinced that Fortes was in the clear.

A few days after Oldham had written, Bottomley himself wrote to the Governor explaining the position. He was worried about the possible repercussions of a refusal to allow the project to go forward, since it was he rather than the Governor who had to face the people and the politicians at home. 'If Fortes was refused admission, there would be a much worse storm, especially at the London School of Economics, than in the case of Kirchhoff [when] the Secretary of State himself had a good deal of trouble over the affair and I know that my stock went down completely in various quarters for obstructiveness.'[37] It was not only apprehension about the protests from the London School of Economics which Malinowski, but principally Richards, had encouraged, but that evidence about Fortes' subversive activities was lacking. Bottomley had arranged for further enquiries to be made and the Colonial Office was told that 'as far as can be ascertained, Fortes takes no part in any subversive propaganda, neither can it be established that he belongs to the Communist Party'. Even at this late stage Oldham was asked to make further enquiries, which he did from Malinowski and Coatman at the London School of Economics. Coatman had had a career in the Indian police and was connected with the Criminal Investigation Department, so his voice carried much weight. He replied that Fortes was 'a man of sensible and balanced views, very easy to get on with, quick to see the humorous side of things, and altogether very much a man to my liking'.[38] Malinowski generously concentrated upon his 'exceptional intellectual gifts'. 'He is an original thinker, an extremely able constructive critic ... he is going to make an exceptionally good field-worker' because he is 'an excellent mixer'. The only qualification he has is that Fortes is still 'very self-conscious' and did not at first make a convincing impression on the Council of the International African Institute. At the end of this long succession of enquiries, the 'wail' from Oldham, as Shenton Thomas called it, did the trick and permission was given for Fortes to go to the Gold Coast to carry out his research.[39] It was not only the wail from Oldham but the fear of an outcry from senior members of a metropolitan university.

Oldham and Malinowski successfully prevented Fortes' views, which were presumably known to Malinowski better than anyone else, from becoming an issue. He told Fortes where his future lay and indicated what he needed to do to ensure it. Fortes did not rock the boat. In fact

he got on well with many members of the administration of the Gold
Coast after his arrival there. It is true that when he had returned to
England and was about to make a second visit in 1935, the Chief
Commissioner of the Northern Territories called for a report, saying
that 'he should not be encouraged to resume his studies in the
Northern Territories until the value of his work *in its bearings on
administrative questions* has been appraised'.[40] Once again the Colonial
Office, in the person of Creasey, took a more liberal attitude than the
local administrators: 'we can hardly close the Northern Territories to
any form of scientific investigation because we are not satisfied that it
would be directly useful to the political administration of the place'. In
fact Fortes did pay some attention to administrative matters. His first
Tallensi paper on marriage laws was published by the Government
Printer in Accra and he clearly had a hand in Kerr's memorandum on
local government among the Frafra, in which category the Tallensi
were included. Kerr was the local District Commissioner working at
Bolgatanga, and Fortes got on well with him and with the Agricultural
Officer, Lynn. During the period of his return to London, when he
attended Malinowski's seminars, evidence of an ambiguous kind came
along of his 'utility' to the authorities in the Gold Coast. For in
November he was written to at length by Canon H. M. Grace, the new
Principal of Achimota College, in very flattering terms, asking him to
join the staff. An anthropologist's help was needed to deal construc-
tively with the restless spirits of the students who found themselves
between two worlds. Fortes was very receptive to this suggestion both
from the 'practical' and from the 'scientific' point of view. As he was
still a Fellow of the International African Institute, he sent them a copy
of this letter, pointing out that such a post would make it possible for
him to pursue the Institute's interests in changing African cultures. But
a copy of the letter was duly despatched by Vischer (again) to the
Colonial Office and hence to Sir Arnold Hodson, the acting Governor
of the Gold Coast. Hodson became very worried, not so much at the
invitation to Fortes as at the tone of Grace's letter. He objected to the
statements that 'this country is in a precarious position in regard to its
future political life' and blamed the bad reputation the Gold Coast had
got on the local press as well as on policy statements to the effect that
we are training Africans to take over the administrative structure.
However the question of the appropriateness of an anthropologist for
such a position, and of Fortes in particular, was inevitably raised.
Hodson consulted his advisors. The Head of the Education Depart-

ment thought that Grace was quite right to be worried about the future and hoped the Government would make a clear statement about its policy, for example, regarding Africans filling 'European' jobs. But he did not think an anthropologist would do the job. Nor did the acting Governor, certainly not in the case of Fortes.[41]

Hodson apparently based his judgement on the earlier correspondence in the file about Fortes and thought him unsuitable for the post. 'He is a South African and married to a Russian wife, and from all accounts has an unprepossessing appearance and no charm of manner.'[42] An additional source of information was Hugh Thomas, younger brother of the Governor, Shenton Thomas, who was now Secretary for Native Affairs and had known of Fortes in the North. When approached by Hodson he, like the Director of Education, was not unsympathetic to Grace's complaint about training people for a fictitious future, nor was he against anthropologists, holding them to be 'a valuable asset in any backward country'. Of Fortes he knew little, except that he was 'a very extreme anthropologist'.[43] By this he meant something quite different from his brother. Far from being over-interested in changing local society, Fortes was criticised for wanting to maintain it – the classic dilemma of the anthropologist, the contradiction of the progressive preservationist, the radical conserver. For 'he would prefer to let the races remain in their natural state. For instance he deprecates the introduction of coinage into the N.T.s [Northern Territories] when the system of barter would be equally beneficial to the native. In fact it does exist in some spots in the N.T.s and that is Fortes' objection, that we are trying to alter it.'

On the same day that he replied to Bottomley at the Colonial Office, the acting Governor sent off a secret telegram to the Chief Commissioner of the Northern Territories asking for information about Fortes' political views, his social, personal qualifications and the value of the work he was doing. The reply was interesting and showed how correct Oldham had been, or alternatively how Fortes' supposed views had been changed by his experiences. His present views were found to be 'more in accord [with] Government policy' while the administrative officers 'like him personally [and] consider his social qualities up to average [while he] has shown readiness [to] give advice when asked and [there is] no reason to think [the] advice unsound or prejudiced'. He added that he had published one article in *Africa*. Much the same assessment was implied in the report of Hugh Thomas, who saw Fortes at the time of the next meeting of the Council of

Achimota School when he spent a month there after leaving England on 18 March 1936. This visit to Achimota had been arranged by the Colonial Office in London before it heard of the Governor's initial objections. When he spoke to Thomas of the job, Fortes said he had first to finish the work in the Northern Territories and in any case would not consider the matter at all, 'unless he had Government's full support'.[44] This seemed to settle the question as far as the acting Governor was concerned. Fortes no longer appeared a threat, indeed was viewed as the possible source of sound advice about future developments.

It should be added that Fortes' views were not as much in accord with many aspects of colonial policy in the Gold Coast as his interlocutors supposed. On the other hand he was very much in tune with the movement that saw education as a means to self-government, that backed the shift from 'Trusteeship' to 'Partnership', especially as it was later embodied in the Colonial Development and Welfare Act of 1940. That proposal replaced the 'conservative' *laissez-faire* policy of colonial rule with a commitment to the positive intervention of the state in increasing the pace of social change. He was very much part of the pre-war group of left-wing intellectuals associated with the Fabian Society who influenced the movement towards colonial independence that took place in Britain in the decade and a half following the Second World War, affecting on the one hand the actions of politicians in the metropolis and on the other giving some support to the growing pressure from the subject populations.

Fortes took 'practical' anthropology seriously, as he had done 'practical' psychology in London's East End. But in this context practical anthropology was understood to be a matter of helping people to adapt to social change rather than promoting those changes themselves. That would have been his role at Achimota and it was certainly one that interested him, but it was to be combined with research. As a result of this visit to the College he wrote a 'Memorandum on social research at Achimota: the need for socio-logical research', which was to have an impact not only on his own career but also on further developments in the Gold Coast.

Despite all that political manoeuvring, the Achimota invitation did bear fruit. Fortes carried out a further year of fieldwork and returned to London in mid-August 1937 by way of South Africa.[45] He applied straight away to the International African Institute to prolong his Fellowship for a further year in order to write up his material. But his original project on the family had been shifted, at least formally, in favour of writing up 'that segment of the culture of the Tallensi which is of most immediate concern to people working in the area, officials and others. Its topic will be the social structure: Local and Kinship grouping: political organization: the economic systems: law and family government.' This statement represents exactly what he did in his two major monographs, although the way in which he carried out the project demonstrates more his changing theoretical interest in 'social structure', following the work of Evans-Pritchard and Firth, rather than any strong impulse to communicate to those 'in the area', who would find his work heavy going if not incomprehensible.[46]

At the same time as he made his application to the Institute, Fortes reported that he had been to see Grace, who told him of an unexpected obstacle in his coming to Achimota. However he asked him to co-operate with his Arts Supervisor (Meyerowitz) 'in drawing up a comprehensive scheme for the establishment of an Institute of West African Culture, for research and teaching in West African sociology and arts and crafts', a project that was then being considered by official bodies both in Britain and the Gold Coast.

The memorandum for this project was drawn up later that year by W. B. Mumford of the Colonial Department of the University of London Institute of Education, who proposed to include as chapter III of his report a contribution by Fortes entitled 'Some notes on the formation of a School of Social Studies at Achimota College'. The proposal was for a Museum, a Research Unit, a Teaching Unit and a Service Unit with applied functions; the Teaching Unit would offer courses at different levels including those at the university now planned for Achimota; the other units would involve the training and recruiting of local staff. The emphasis would be on facing the problem of the 'transition mentality'.[47] As things turned out, the project did not get off the ground before war began, in less than two years' time. One way and another Fortes had to seek other means of support. He held a number of temporary jobs while he was writing up his material and planning *African Political Systems* with Evans-Pritchard, a project submitted to the same 16th meeting of the Executive Committee as his application for an extension. At the same time Evans-Pritchard, who for some years had had a job at Oxford where in 1937 Radcliffe-Brown had taken up the first Chair in Social Anthropology (and was about to give his first seminar), wrote to say how much Brown (i.e. Radcliffe-Brown) would like to have him there as well. 'With R.-B., you, and me

we would have quite a decent nucleus for a school.'[48] But the hoped-
for post at Oxford did not materialise and Fortes had to take a year's
appointment at the London School of Economics for 1938–9. Nevertheless the trio was always looking forward to getting together later and
in a sense *African Political Systems*, with the Preface by Radcliffe-Brown
and the Introduction by Fortes and Evans-Pritchard, is a memorial to
their collaboration, hoped-for and later achieved, including as it does
contributions by their allies, Max Gluckman and Isaac Schapera.

The Achimota project remained on the books and was revived
towards the end of the war. Fortes, who had spent the latter years of
the war in Nigeria and Ghana, partly on intelligence work, wrote
another memorandum on the proposed Institute in 1943, entitled 'The
West African Institute of Arts, Industries and Social Sciences: notes on
policy', which refers specifically to Grace's work eight years before and
includes the name of Mr Meyerowitz, the Arts Supervisor at Achimota
and an important influence on modern artistic developments in West
Africa. The plan for this Institute, although still in association with
Achimota, was much more ambitious than the previous scheme, a
scope clearly influenced by Fortes' wartime participation in Lord
Hailey's investigations in Nigeria, where he first went from Oxford
before carrying out intelligence work on the border of the Vichy-held
territories. It was to be established on a West African basis, and the
long-term plans included a comprehensive ethnographic survey, as well
as work on local agriculture, political systems, cash crops, new
industries and an enquiry preparing the way for a town plan for Accra.
Later in the same year, he submitted a memorandum to the
Commission on Higher Education in West Africa on setting up a new
University of which the Institute would form a part. Its establishment
was once again supported by the new Principal of Achimota, the Revd
R. A. Stopford, later Bishop of London, who became chairman of the
management committee. Further general support came from missionary circles, strongly associated with Achimota, and particularly
from the energetic Oldham of the International African Institute. The
whole venture now became possible because of the changing policy of
the metropolitan government towards colonial development as embodied in the Colonial Development and Welfare Act of 1940, the
provision of which supported much post-war research. The Second
World War represented a decisive turning point in the history of
colonial empires, partly as a result of the coalition government, the war
itself and the leftist ideologies that were promoted to support it, partly

because of changing public conceptions at home and partly because of greater pressures from below and the concessions needed to secure local support in wartime. Each of the factors had important influences on the development in social anthropology in Britain.

How far was the direction of Fortes' research influenced by the suppliers of funds and the providers of permits? A bow was certainly made to the wishes of the Rockefeller philanthropies for work on 'culture contact', but it was little more than that. A contribution was made to the reorganisation of Tallensi local government, while a paper on marriage was published by the Government Printing Press. Basically the latter were uninterested in his work, in which they saw little value. Of Malinowski's teaching something remained, but basically Fortes' agenda was set in discussions with his peers, and specifically with Evans-Pritchard. The written analysis of his fieldwork owes most to Firth and Evans-Pritchard, but it was also Radcliffe-Brown whom he looked upon as his real guru. That meant setting on one side some of his psychological interests, but they returned later with renewed force. Meanwhile it was undoubtedly his friendship with Evans-Pritchard that led him in a sociological direction.

CHAPTER 4

Personal and intellectual friendships: Fortes and Evans-Pritchard

To see the work of British anthropologists of the 1930s, even in Africa, as being largely under Malinowski's patronage is correct. Most of the early teachers of the post-war period had worked with him. But that does not mean to imply that they were passive followers or that subgroups did not form within the tribe. Such differentiation took place early on, the friendships and animosities leading to a physical separation (Oxford from the LSE) as well as to a theoretical parting of the ways as between Malinowski's functionalism and Radcliffe-Brown's structuralism, which brought the work closer to that of the French sociological school under Durkheim. It was the latter that gradually achieved dominance but only after Malinowski's death in 1942. That is the story behind the next three chapters.[1]

I have outlined the events that led to Fortes shifting his focus of interest from psychology to anthropology. Intellectual concerns had moved him in that direction following his involvement in studies of children and adolescents in a deprived area of the East End at a time of world depression. But symbolically and actually the shift was carried out as a result of his encounter with the anthropologist Malinowski, at the house of the psychologist, Flügel. That led to his meeting other members of the seminar, of whom the most important for him were the later arrivals, Siegfried Nadel who came from Berlin to take up a Fellowship at the Institute, Raymond Firth, who returned from Sydney early in 1933, but above all an anthropologist who was already marginal to the seminar, Edward Evans-Pritchard.

From the very beginning Evans-Pritchard's relation with Fortes was one of intellectual companionship. Long before Fortes had done any fieldwork, Evans-Pritchard recommended him for a position involving starting a Department of Psychology at the University of Cairo, where he himself was teaching at the time. That was in the first letter he sent,